ONE STOCK
A HUNDRED
SOUPS

ONE STOCK A HUNDRED SOUPS

Linda Doeser

This edition published by Parragon Books Ltd in 2013
LOVE FOOD is an imprint of Parragon Books Ltd

Parragon Books Ltd
Chartist House
15–17 Trim Street
Bath BA1 1HA, UK
www.parragon.com/lovefood

ISBN 978-1-4723-3019-2

Printed in China

Written by Linda Doeser
Internal design by Simon Levy
Cover design by Geoff Borin
Photography by Mike Cooper
Home economy by Lincoln Jefferson

Notes for the Reader
This book uses both metric and imperial measurements. Follow the same units of measurement
throughout; do not mix metric and imperial. All spoon measurements are level: teaspoons are
assumed to be 5 ml, and tablespoons are assumed to be 15 ml. Unless otherwise stated, milk is
assumed to be full fat, eggs and individual vegetables are medium, and pepper is freshly ground
black pepper. Unless otherwise stated, all root vegetables should be washed in plain water and
peeled prior to using.

For best results, use a food thermometer when cooking meat and poultry – check the latest
government guidelines for current advice. Garnishes, decorations and serving suggestions are
all optional and not necessarily included in the recipe ingredients or method. The times given are
an approximate guide only. Preparation times differ according to the techniques used by different
people and the cooking times may also vary from those given. Optional ingredients, variations or
serving suggestions have not been included in the time calculations.

Recipes using raw or very lightly cooked eggs should be avoided by infants, the elderly, pregnant
women, convalescents and anyone suffering from an illness. Pregnant and breastfeeding women are
advised to avoid eating peanuts and peanut products. Sufferers from nut allergies should be aware
that some of the ready-made ingredients used in the recipes in this book may contain nuts. Always
check the packaging before use.

Contents

Introduction

It must have been a great, if unsung moment in the history of civilization when one of our enterprising prehistoric ancestors first put some roots and aromatics into a pot of water and heated it over a fire. Although today's cooking methods are rather less primitive and ingredients are more sophisticated and varied, soup remains one of the easiest dishes to prepare, while still being tasty, nourishing, versatile, easy to digest and the ultimate comfort food.

Soups may be served hot or chilled, they can be a first course or a meal-in-a bowl, they may be hearty and rustic, elegant and subtle, thick and creamy or delicate and clear and can incorporate almost every imaginable ingredient from meat and poultry to vegetables and fruit and from cheese and eggs to fish and shellfish. Virtually every cuisine in the world features at least one – and usually many – soup recipes based on local ingredients and preferences.

The hundred recipes in this book celebrate the immense versatility of soup. Whatever your taste and whatever the occasion, you are sure to find a recipe to suit you. If you're looking for a first course for a dinner party, try Stylish Soups with its collection of clear broths and special flavours or, if it's summer time, Cool Soups with both familiar and unusual chilled delights.

Hearty Soups offers a profusion of great ideas for economical yet satisfying family meals, while Tasty Soups are perfect winter warmers and restoratives for anyone feeling under the weather. For an international flavour, turn to World Classics, which features recipes as varied as a simple yet delicious Greek egg and lemon soup, an unusual sweet and sour onion soup from Iran, Thailand's spicy signature dish Tom Yam Goong and a chicken soup from the United States. All of the recipes are easy to follow, many of them are surprisingly quick to prepare, all of them taste fabulous and, best of all, they are all based on one stock (see page 10).

Making and adapting stock

Obviously, any soup can be made using water as the basic liquid and a few fairly unusual recipes always are. However, as a general rule, the flavour is enriched and intensified with a good-quality stock, which also adds to the nutritional value and helps give 'eye appeal'. Stock can be made from many different ingredients, and restaurant kitchens will have at least a basic collection of chicken, beef and possibly other meat, fish, shellfish and vegetable stocks on hand. This would be demanding for even the most enthusiastic home cook and as most of us are preparing only family meals, an entire freezer would have to be allocated to their storage.

Vegetable stock has been chosen as the basis of the soups in this book for a variety of reasons. It is relatively unusual for any soup, whether featuring chicken, meat, fish, mushrooms, sausages or whatever, not to include some vegetables so it will always go well with other ingredients. Of course some of the best-loved soups are, in any case, vegetable broths. While it is flavourful, it is not so strong that it will overpower other delicate ingredients. It is acceptable to both meat-eaters and vegetarians. Finally, it is easier, more economical and quicker to make a tasty vegetable stock than any other type.

The basic recipe is for what is known as a light stock, meaning its colour not its flavour, and it is suitable for all the soups in the book (and many others). The ingredients are widely available and inexpensive, but you can substitute other vegetables if you like because you particularly dislike one ingredient, you have others to hand or you want to enhance the flavour of a special soup for a particular occasion. All members of the onion family can be used, as well as those suggested. Both fresh and dried mushrooms will add an earthy flavour that some people relish, while others appreciate the sweetness imparted by sweetcorn. However, some vegetables should be used with caution. Any members of the cabbage family, including Brussels sprouts and kohlrabi, are likely to overpower other flavours. Fennel has a distinctive aniseed flavour that won't go with everything but works well with fish and shellfish soups.

Leftover cooked vegetables have neither the flavour nor the nutritional content for making a good stock, but you can make beneficial use of some trimmings. Beware of the cabbage family again and avoid onion skins which can make the stock bitter, but the outer leaves of lettuce, broccoli and cauliflower, mushroom stalks, chard stems and trimmings from asparagus spears and green beans will all add extra flavour – and at no extra cost. Sometimes, the water in which vegetables have been cooked can be substituted for some of the water in the recipe – that from cooking asparagus, broccoli, cauliflower, chard, corn cobs and green beans, for example.

The basic recipe can easily be adapted to make a brown stock which has a deeper flavour and colour and is especially suitable for meat soups. Substitute 2–3 large tomatoes for the potato, parsnips and turnip. Cook the onion, leeks, celery and carrots over a very low heat, stirring occasionally, for about 30 minutes, until they are a rich golden brown. Meanwhile, grill the halved tomatoes until they are golden brown. Add the tomatoes in step 2 with the herbs.

Whatever vegetables you use for the stock and however you cook it, it is advisable not to season it with salt during cooking. As the stock becomes more concentrated, it can become unpleasantly salty. There is an even greater risk of this if you concentrate the stock even more later. Adding salt is best left until you make the soup. This also applies to the addition of spices.

For clarifying stock to make jewel-clear broths, see Jellied Vegetable Consommé (page 165).

As stock can be stored in the freezer for up to 3 months, it is worth making a large batch. Freeze it in measured quantities, such as 500 ml/18 fl oz, so it is easy to remove the amount you need to use for a particular soup.

So as the temperature drops outside in those long winter months, delicious and nutritious soups can be quickly and easily created for instant warmth. Whether you are entertaining guests, feeding the family or need something tasty to serve at an impromptu gathering, soup wins every time – your only problem will be choosing which one to serve!

Basic Vegetable Stock

This is the recipe that all 100 variations of soup in the book are based on. For each recipe the basic stock is highlighted (✳) for easy reference, so then all you have to do is follow the easy steps each time and a world of delicious and delectable soups will await you.

Makes 1 litre/ 1¾ pints

✳ 2 tbsp sunflower oil
✳ 1 onion, finely chopped
✳ 2 leeks, thinly sliced
✳ 2 celery sticks, finely chopped
✳ 1 large potato, diced
✳ 2 carrots, thinly sliced

✳ 2 small parsnips, thinly sliced
✳ 1 small turnip, thinly sliced
✳ 2 bay leaves
✳ 6 fresh parsley sprigs
✳ 150 ml/5 fl oz dry white wine
✳ 1 litre/1¾ pints water

1 Heat the oil in a large saucepan. Add the onion, leeks, celery and potato and cook over a low heat, stirring frequently, for about 8 minutes, until softened and just beginning to colour.

2 Add the carrots, parsnips, turnip, bay leaves, parsley sprigs and white wine, stir well and cook for 2 minutes, until the alcohol has evaporated. Increase the heat to medium, pour in the water and bring to the boil. Reduce the heat, cover and simmer for 1 hour.

3 Remove the pan from the heat and strain the stock into a bowl through a fine sieve, pressing the vegetables with the back of a ladle to extract as much liquid as possible; do not press the vegetables through the sieve. Strain again and leave to cool completely, then cover with clingfilm and store in the refrigerator for up to 2 days. Alternatively, freeze for up to 3 months.

Hearty

Summer Tomato Soup

1. Heat the olive oil in a large, heavy-based saucepan. Add the onion, spring onions, garlic and celery and cook over a low heat, stirring occasionally, for 5 minutes, until softened. Add the tomatoes, cover and simmer, stirring occasionally, for 50 minutes, until thickened.

2. Remove the pan from the heat and leave to cool slightly. Transfer the mixture to a food processor or blender, in batches if necessary, and process to a smooth purée, then pass the purée through a strainer into a clean saucepan.

3. Add the stock and bring to the boil, stirring constantly. Season to taste with cayenne, salt and pepper, add the pasta and bring back to the boil. Boil over a medium heat for 8–10 minutes, until the pasta is tender, but still firm to the bite.

4. Meanwhile, make the garnish. Melt the butter in a small frying pan. Add the parsley sprigs, in batches, and cook for a few seconds, then turn and cook for a few seconds more. Remove from the pan and drain on kitchen paper.

5. Taste the soup and adjust the seasoning, if necessary. Ladle into warmed bowls, sprinkle with the fried parsley and serve immediately.

Serves 6

3 tbsp olive oil

1 large onion, finely chopped

4 spring onions, finely chopped

3 garlic cloves, finely chopped

2 celery sticks, finely chopped

800 g/ 1 lb 12 oz tomatoes, peeled and chopped

700 ml/1¼ pints basic vegetable stock

pinch of cayenne pepper

85 g/3 oz stellette or other small pasta shapes

salt and pepper

To garnish
85 g/3 oz unsalted butter

12 fresh parsley sprigs

Tomato & White Bean Soup

1. Heat the olive oil in a large saucepan. Add the onions, celery, red pepper and garlic and cook over a low heat, stirring occasionally, for 5 minutes, until softened.

2. Increase the heat to medium, add the tomatoes and cook, stirring occasionally, for a further 5 minutes, then pour in the stock. Stir in the tomato purée, sugar and sweet paprika and season to taste with salt and pepper. Bring to the boil, reduce the heat and simmer for 15 minutes.

3. Meanwhile, mash together the butter and flour to a paste in a small bowl with a fork. Stir the paste, in small pieces at a time, into the soup. Make sure each piece is fully incorporated before adding the next.

4. Add the beans, stir well and simmer for a further 5 minutes, until heated through. Sprinkle with the parsley and serve immediately.

Serves 6

3 tbsp olive oil

450 g/1 lb red onions, chopped

1 celery stick with leaves, chopped

1 red pepper, deseeded and chopped

2 garlic cloves, finely chopped

1 kg/2 lb 4 oz plum tomatoes, peeled and chopped

1.3 litres/2¼ pints basic vegetable stock

2 tbsp tomato purée

1 tsp sugar

1 tbsp sweet paprika

1 tbsp butter

1 tbsp plain flour

400 g/14 oz canned cannellini beans, drained and rinsed

salt and pepper

3 tbsp chopped fresh flat-leaf parsley, to garnish

Barley, Lentil & Onion Soup

1. Put the barley into a large saucepan, pour in the water and bring to the boil. Reduce the heat, cover and simmer gently, stirring frequently, for about 30 minutes, until all the liquid has been absorbed.

2. Add the stock, onions, lentils, ginger and cumin and bring to the boil over a medium heat. Reduce the heat, cover and simmer, stirring occasionally, for 1½ hours, adding a little more stock if necessary.

3. Meanwhile, make the garnish. Spread out the onions on a thick layer of kitchen paper and cover with another thick layer. Leave to dry out for 30 minutes. Heat the oil in a frying pan. Add the onions and cook over a low heat, stirring constantly, for about 20 minutes, until well browned. Add the garlic and cook, stirring constantly, for a further 5 minutes. Remove the onions with a slotted spoon and drain well on kitchen paper.

4. Season the soup to taste with salt and pepper, stir in the lemon juice and coriander and simmer for a further 5 minutes. Serve immediately, garnished with the browned onions.

Serves 6

25 g/1 oz pearl barley

150 ml/5 fl oz water

1.7 litres/3 pints basic vegetable stock

500 g/1 lb 2 oz onions, thinly sliced into rings

140 g/5 oz Puy lentils

½ tsp ground ginger

1 tsp ground cumin

3 tbsp lemon juice

2 tbsp chopped fresh coriander

salt and pepper

To garnish

2 onions, halved and thinly sliced

5 tbsp vegetable oil

2 garlic cloves, finely chopped

Green Vegetable Soup

1. Pour the stock into a saucepan and bring to the boil. Meanwhile, heat the oil in a large saucepan. Add the leeks and cook over a low heat, stirring occasionally, for 5 minutes, until softened, then remove the pan from the heat.

2. Stir in the flour until fully incorporated, then gradually stir in the hot stock, a little at a time. Season with salt and pepper and add the thyme and fennel seeds.

3. Return the pan to the heat and bring to the boil, stirring constantly. Add the lettuce, spinach, peas, watercress and mint and bring back to the boil. Boil, stirring constantly, for 3–4 minutes, then reduce the heat, cover and simmer gently for 30 minutes.

4. Remove the soup from the heat and leave to cool slightly. Ladle it into a food processor or blender, in batches if necessary, and process to a smooth purée. Return the soup to the rinsed-out pan and reheat, stirring occasionally. When it is piping hot, ladle into warmed bowls, sprinkle with the parsley and serve with garlic and herb bread.

Serves 6

- 1.5 litres/2¾ pints basic vegetable stock
- 3 tbsp olive oil
- 2 leeks, white parts only, chopped
- 2 tbsp plain flour
- 1 tsp dried thyme
- ½ tsp fennel seeds
- 1 Little Gem lettuce, roughly chopped
- 500 g/1 lb 2 oz spinach, coarse stalks removed
- 280 g/10 oz shelled fresh or frozen peas
- 1 bunch of watercress or rocket
- 4 tbsp chopped fresh mint
- salt and pepper
- 2 tbsp chopped fresh flat-leaf parsley, to garnish
- garlic and herb bread, toasted, to serve

Squash & Lentil Soup

1. Heat the oil in a large saucepan. Add the onions and garlic and cook over a low heat, stirring occasionally, for 5 minutes, until softened. Add the cumin, cinnamon, nutmeg, ginger and coriander and cook, stirring constantly, for 1 minute.

2. Stir in the pumpkin and lentils and cook, stirring constantly for 2 minutes, then pour in the stock and bring to the boil over a medium heat. Reduce the heat and simmer, stirring occasionally, for 50–60 minutes, until the vegetables are tender.

3. Remove from the heat and leave to cool slightly, then ladle into a food processor or blender, in batches if necessary, and process to a smooth purée.

4. Return the soup to the rinsed-out pan, stir in the lemon juice, season to taste with salt and pepper and reheat gently. Ladle into warmed bowls, top with a swirl of crème fraîche and serve.

Serves 6

3 tbsp olive oil

2 large onions, chopped

2 garlic cloves, chopped

2 tsp ground cumin

1 tsp ground cinnamon

½ tsp freshly grated nutmeg

½ tsp ground ginger

½ tsp ground coriander

1 kg/2 lb 4 oz pumpkin or butternut squash, deseeded and cut into small chunks

350 g/12 oz red or yellow lentils

1.7 litres/3 pints basic vegetable stock

3 tbsp lemon juice

salt and pepper

crème fraîche or Greek-style yogurt, to garnish

Ribollita

1. Put half the beans into a food processor or blender and process briefly to a coarse purée. Scrape into a bowl and set aside.

2. Heat the oil in a large saucepan. Add the onion, leek, garlic, carrots and celery and cook over a low heat, stirring occasionally, for 8–10 minutes. Add the potatoes and courgettes and cook, stirring constantly, for 2 minutes.

3. Add the tomatoes, tomato paste and dried chilli, if using, and cook, stirring constantly, for 3 minutes, then stir in the bean purée. Cook, stirring constantly, for 2 minutes more.

4. Pour in the stock and add the cavolo nero and Savoy cabbage. Bring to the boil, reduce the heat and simmer for 2 hours.

5. Meanwhile, preheat the grill. Rub the bread with the halved garlic cloves and toast on both sides.

6. Stir the whole beans into the soup and heat through gently for 10 minutes. Season with salt and pepper. Put the garlic-flavoured bread in the base of warmed soup bowls and ladle the soup over it. Drizzle with a little olive oil and serve immediately.

Serves 6

400 g/14 oz canned haricot or cannellini beans, drained and rinsed

3 tbsp olive oil, plus extra for drizzling

1 Spanish onion, chopped

1 leek, chopped

4 garlic cloves, finely chopped

2 carrots, diced

2 celery sticks, chopped

2 potatoes, diced

2 courgettes, diced

2 large tomatoes, peeled, deseeded and chopped

1 tsp sun-dried tomato paste

1 dried chilli, crushed (optional)

1.7 litres/3 pints basic vegetable stock

225 g/8 oz cavolo nero (Tuscan cabbage), shredded

225 g/8 oz Savoy cabbage, shredded

6 slices of ciabatta

2 garlic cloves, halved

salt and pepper

Bacon & Potato Soup

1. Heat the olive oil in a large saucepan. Add the bacon, onions and garlic and cook over a medium heat, stirring frequently, for 5–7 minutes, until the bacon is crisp and the onions are lightly browned.

2. Pour in the stock and add the potatoes, cabbage, Worcestershire sauce and mustard, season with pepper to taste and mix well. Bring to the boil, then reduce the heat and simmer, stirring occasionally, for 30 minutes.

3. Remove the pan from the heat and leave to cool slightly, then transfer 600 ml/1 pint to a food processor or blender. Process briefly to a coarse purée and return to the pan. Stir well and return the soup to the heat. Cook, stirring frequently, for 5–10 minutes, until heated through. Season with salt to taste, stir in the parsley and ladle into warmed bowls. Serve immediately with wholemeal rolls.

Serves 6

2 tbsp olive oil

175 g/6 oz lean bacon, chopped

2 onions, chopped

2 garlic cloves, finely chopped

1.7 litres/3 pints basic vegetable stock

650 g/1 lb 7 oz potatoes, diced

280 g/10 oz Savoy cabbage, shredded

1 tsp Worcestershire or Tabasco sauce

1 tsp Dijon mustard

3 tbsp finely chopped fresh parsley

salt and pepper

wholemeal rolls, to serve

Pork Soup with Bulgar Wheat

1. Heat the oil in a large pan. Add the pork, onions and garlic, if using, and cook over a medium heat, stirring occasionally, for 8 minutes, until the meat is lightly browned.

2. Pour in the wine and cook, stirring constantly, for 2 minutes, until the alcohol has evaporated, then pour in the stock. Reduce the heat, cover and simmer for 15 minutes.

3. Add the bulgar wheat, season to taste with salt and pepper and cook for a further 15 minutes, until the meat and wheat are tender and the soup has thickened.

4. Stir in the lemon juice. Taste and adjust the seasoning, if necessary. Serve the soup immediately, sprinkled with a little cayenne pepper and accompanied by soda bread.

Serves 4–6

5 tbsp olive oil

500 g/1 lb 2 oz boneless pork, diced

2 onions, chopped

2 garlic cloves, finely chopped (optional)

125 ml/4 fl oz white wine

1.4 litres/2½ pints basic vegetable stock

200 g/7 oz bulgar wheat

3 tbsp lemon juice

salt and pepper

pinch of cayenne pepper, to garnish

soda bread, to serve

Salt Pork & Lentil Soup

1. Put the salt pork into a large saucepan and cook over medium heat, stirring frequently, for 8–10 minutes, until it has released most of its fat and is browned all over. Remove from the pan with a slotted spoon and drain on kitchen paper. Set aside.

2. Add the oil to the pan and heat. Add the onion, garlic and potatoes and cook over a low heat, stirring occasionally, for 5 minutes, until the onion has softened. Stir in the lentils and cook, stirring constantly, for 5 minutes.

3. Pour in the stock, increase the heat to medium, add the bouquet garni and bring to the boil, stirring constantly. Reduce the heat, cover and simmer for 1½–2 hours, until the lentils are very soft. Stir in the salt pork, season to taste with salt and pepper, and cook, stirring occasionally, for a further 10 minutes, until heated through.

4. Remove the pan from the heat. Remove and discard the bouquet garni. Pour the soup into a warmed tureen and serve immediately with crusty bread.

Serves 6–8

225 g/8 oz salt pork, diced

2 tbsp olive oil

1 onion, chopped

3 garlic cloves, finely chopped

4 potatoes, diced

500 g/1 lb 2 oz red lentils

2 litres/3½ pints basic vegetable stock

1 bouquet garni (1 bay leaf, 1 fresh thyme sprig and 3 fresh parsley sprigs, tied together)

salt and pepper

crusty bread, to serve

Mixed Vegetable Soup with Lamb Meatballs

1. Put the onions, celeriac, swede, carrots, potatoes, red peppers, tomatoes, peas and lemon slices into a large saucepan, pour in the stock and season with salt and pepper. Bring to the boil, then reduce the heat, cover and simmer for 25–30 minutes.

2. Meanwhile, make the meatballs. Mix together the lamb, parsley and rice in a bowl, kneading well until thoroughly combined. Season with salt and pepper. Break off pieces of the mixture, about the size of golf balls, and shape them into balls between the palms of your hand. Dust with flour, shaking off the excess.

3. Add the meatballs to the soup, re-cover the pan and cook, stirring occasionally, for a further 40–45 minutes. Serve immediately.

Serves 6

2 onions, finely chopped

1 small celeriac, diced

½ swede, diced

3 carrots, diced

2 potatoes, diced

2 red peppers, deseeded and diced

4 tomatoes, peeled, deseeded and chopped

115 g/4 oz shelled fresh or frozen peas

1 lemon, sliced

1.5 litres/2¾ pints basic vegetable stock

salt and pepper

Lamb meatballs

350 g/12 oz minced lamb

3 tbsp chopped fresh parsley

70 g/2½ oz medium-grain rice

plain flour, for dusting

salt and pepper

Beef Noodle Soup

1. Put the dried mushrooms into a bowl, pour in boiling water to cover and leave to soak for 20 minutes. If using Chinese mushrooms, drain and rinse. If using porcini, drain, reserving the soaking water. Strain the soaking water through a fine sieve or coffee filter paper into a bowl.

2. Heat the oil in a large saucepan. Add the strips of beef and cook, stirring constantly, until browned all over. Remove with a slotted spoon and drain on kitchen paper.

3. Add the carrots, spring onions, garlic and ginger to the pan and cook, stirring constantly, for 5 minutes. Return the beef to the pan, pour in the stock and add the soy sauce, hoisin sauce and rice wine. Add the mushrooms and porcini soaking water, if using. Season with pepper and bring to the boil over a medium heat, then reduce the heat and simmer for 15 minutes.

4. Add the noodles and spinach to the pan, stir well and simmer for a further 7–8 minutes. Taste and add more pepper or soy sauce, if necessary. Serve immediately.

Serves 6

15 g/½ oz dried Chinese mushrooms or porcini mushrooms

3 tbsp corn oil

500 g/1 lb 2 oz lean beef, such as fillet or sirloin, cut into thin strips

175 g/6 oz carrots, cut into julienne strips

10 spring onions, finely shredded

2 garlic cloves, finely chopped

2.5-cm/1-inch piece fresh ginger, finely chopped

1.7 litres/3 pints basic vegetable stock

4 tbsp dark soy sauce

1 tbsp hoisin sauce

6 tbsp Chinese rice wine or dry sherry

140 g/5 oz egg noodles

140 g/5 oz shredded spinach

pepper

Split Pea & Sausage Soup

1. Put the pork into a large saucepan and pour in the stock. Add the onion, leeks, carrots, celery, apple, peas, bouquet garni and treacle and bring to the boil. Using a skimmer or slotted spoon, skim off any scum that rises to the surface, then reduce the heat, cover and simmer, stirring occasionally, for 2 hours.

2. Season the soup to taste with salt and pepper and remove and discard the bouquet garni. Stir in the butter and sausages and simmer for a further 5 minutes. Serve immediately with rye bread.

Serves 6

175 g/6 oz boneless belly of pork, cut into cubes

2 litres/3½ pints basic vegetable stock

1 onion, chopped

4 leeks, chopped

3 carrots, chopped

3 celery sticks, chopped

1 tart eating apple, peeled, cored and chopped

375 g/13 oz split peas, soaked overnight in cold water to cover, drained and rinsed

1 bouquet garni (2 fresh parsley sprigs, 1 fresh thyme sprig and 1 fresh mint sprig)

1 tbsp treacle

2 tbsp butter

4 bockwurst, Wienerwurst or frankfurters, cut into 2.5-cm/1-inch lengths

salt and pepper

crusty rye bread, to serve

Sauerkraut & Sausage Soup

1. Melt the butter in a large saucepan over a low heat. Add the flour and paprika and cook, stirring constantly, for 2 minutes, then remove the pan from the heat. Gradually stir in the stock, a little at a time, until fully incorporated and the mixture is smooth.

2. Return the pan to medium heat and bring to the boil, stirring constantly. Add the sauerkraut and sausages and season with salt and pepper. Reduce the heat, cover and simmer for 30 minutes.

3. Meanwhile, make the dumplings. Sift together the flour and salt into a bowl. Beat the egg in another bowl, then gradually beat in the dry ingredients, a little at a time. Turn out on to a floured surface and knead until smooth. Cover and leave to rest for 15 minutes.

4. Divide the dough into 6 pieces and roll into sausage shapes. Flour your hands, pinch off pieces of the dough and add to the soup. Re-cover the pan and simmer for a further 5 minutes. Remove the pan from the heat, stir in the soured cream and serve immediately.

Serves 6

2 tbsp butter

1 tbsp plain flour

1 tbsp sweet paprika

2 litres/3½ pints basic vegetable stock

650 g/1 lb 7 oz sauerkraut, drained

500 g/1 lb 2 oz smoked pork sausages, cut into 2.5-cm/1-inch slices

150 ml/5 fl oz soured cream

salt and pepper

Dumplings

85 g/3 oz strong white bread flour, plus extra for dusting

pinch of salt

1 large egg

Chicken & Lentil Soup

1. Heat the oil in a large saucepan. Add the onion, leeks, carrots, celery and mushrooms and cook over a low heat, stirring occasionally, for 5–7 minutes, until softened but not coloured.

2. Increase the heat to medium, pour in the wine and cook for 2–3 minutes, until the alcohol has evaporated, then pour in the stock. Bring to the boil, add the bay leaf and herbs, reduce the heat, cover and simmer for 30 minutes.

3. Add the lentils, re-cover the pan and simmer, stirring occasionally, for a further 40 minutes, until they are tender.

4. Stir in the chicken, season to taste with salt and pepper and simmer for a further 5–10 minutes, until heated through. Serve immediately.

Serves 6

3 tbsp olive oil

1 large onion, chopped

2 leeks, chopped

2 carrots, chopped

2 celery sticks, chopped

175 g/6 oz button mushrooms, chopped

4 tbsp dry white wine

1.2 litres/2 pints basic vegetable stock

1 bay leaf

2 tsp dried mixed herbs

175 g/6 oz Puy lentils

350 g/12 oz boneless cooked chicken, diced

salt and pepper

Chicken Soup with Matzo Balls

1. First, make the matzo balls. Melt 1 tablespoon of the butter in a small frying pan. Add the onion and cook over a low heat, stirring occasionally, for 5 minutes, until softened. Remove from the heat and leave to cool.

2. Beat the remaining butter in a bowl until fluffy, then gradually beat in the egg and egg yolk. Add the parsley and onion, season with salt and pepper and mix well, then beat in the water. Mix in the matzo crumbs until thoroughly incorporated. Cover and leave to rest in the refrigerator for 30 minutes.

3. Meanwhile, put the chicken into a large saucepan and pour in the stock. Bring to the boil over a medium–low heat, skimming off the scum that rises to the surface. Simmer for 15 minutes.

4. Add the onions, celery, carrots, tomatoes and parsley and season with salt and pepper. Reduce the heat, cover and simmer for 50–60 minutes, until the chicken is cooked through and tender. Meanwhile, shape the matzo mixture into 18 balls.

5. Strain the soup into a clean pan, reserving the chicken quarters. Remove and discard the skin and bones and cut the meat into bite-sized pieces. Add the chicken, vermicelli and matzo balls to the pan, cover and simmer gently for 20–30 minutes. Serve immediately, garnished with chopped parsley.

Serves 6

2 chicken quarters

2.5 litres/4½ pints basic vegetable stock

2 onions, chopped

2 celery sticks, chopped

2 carrots, chopped

2 tomatoes, peeled and chopped

2 fresh parsley sprigs

55 g/2 oz vermicelli

salt and pepper

chopped fresh parsley, to garnish

Matzo balls

55 g/2 oz butter

½ onion, grated

1 egg

1 egg yolk

1 tbsp finely chopped fresh parsley

1 tbsp water

115 g/4 oz matzo crackers, crushed

salt and pepper

Chicken & Almond Soup

1. Melt the butter in a saucepan. Add the leeks and ginger and cook over a low heat, stirring occasionally, for 5 minutes, until softened. Add the chicken, carrots, peas, chillies and ground almonds and cook, stirring constantly, for 10 minutes.

2. Stir in the coriander, remove from the heat and leave to cool slightly. Spoon the chicken mixture into a food processor or blender and process until very finely chopped. Add the stock and process to a purée.

3. Return the mixture to the pan, season to taste with salt and pepper and bring to the boil. Reduce the heat to very low and gradually stir in the cream; do not let the soup come back to the boil. Simmer, stirring frequently, for 2 minutes. Ladle into warmed bowls, sprinkle with chopped coriander and Parmesan and serve.

Serves 6

115 g/4 oz butter

2 leeks, chopped

2-cm/¾-inch piece of fresh ginger, finely chopped

175 g/6 oz skinless, boneless chicken, diced

2 carrots, chopped

85 g/3 oz shelled fresh or frozen peas

2 green chillies, deseeded and chopped

140 g/5 oz ground almonds

1 tbsp chopped fresh coriander, plus extra to garnish

700 ml/1¼ pints basic vegetable stock

350 ml/12 fl oz single cream

salt and pepper

grated Parmesan cheese, to serve

17

Chicken Soup with Leeks & Rice

1. Heat the oil in a saucepan. Add the leeks and cook over a low heat, stirring occasionally, for 5 minutes, until softened. Add the chicken, increase the heat to medium and cook, stirring frequently, for 2 minutes. Add the rice and cook, stirring constantly, for 2 minutes more.

2. Pour in the stock, add the Worcestershire sauce and chives and bring to the boil. Reduce the heat, cover and simmer for 20–25 minutes.

3. Meanwhile, preheat the grill. Grill the bacon for 2–4 minutes on each side, until crisp. Remove and leave to cool, then crumble.

4. Season the soup to taste with salt and pepper and stir in the parsley. Ladle into warmed bowls, sprinkle with the crumbled bacon and serve.

Serves 6

2 tbsp olive oil

3 leeks, chopped

6 skinless, boneless chicken thighs, diced

55 g/2 oz long-grain rice

1.3 litres/2¼ pints basic vegetable stock

dash of Worcestershire sauce

6 fresh chives, chopped

6 thin bacon rashers

2 tbsp chopped fresh parsley

salt and pepper

Fish Soup with Semolina & Dill Dumplings

1. Put the chorizo into a heavy-based saucepan and cook over a medium–low heat, stirring frequently, for 5 minutes until lightly browned. Add the fish and cook, occasionally stirring gently, for 2 minutes.

2. Sprinkle in the paprika and cayenne pepper, pour in the stock and bring to the boil. Reduce the heat, cover and simmer for 10 minutes.

3. Add the potatoes, tomatoes and parsley, stir gently, re-cover the pan and simmer for 10 minutes.

4. Meanwhile, make the semolina and dill dumplings. Mix together the semolina, salt and dill in a bowl. Lightly beat together the egg and milk in another bowl, then stir into the dry ingredients until thoroughly combined. Cover and leave to rest in the refrigerator for 10 minutes.

5. Scoop up tablespoonfuls of the dumpling mixture and add them to the soup. Re-cover the pan and simmer for a further 10 minutes. Season to taste with salt and pepper and serve immediately.

Serves 6

85 g/3 oz chorizo, diced

500 g/1 lb 2 oz white fish fillets, skinned and diced

1 tbsp sweet paprika

pinch of cayenne pepper

1.4 litres/2½ pints basic vegetable stock

4 potatoes, diced

4 tomatoes, peeled and diced

1 tbsp chopped fresh parsley

salt and pepper

Semolina & dill dumplings
85 g/3 oz fine semolina

pinch of salt

1 tbsp chopped fresh dill

1 egg

3 tbsp milk

Fish & Sweet Potato Soup

1. Put the fish, sweet potato, onion, carrots and cinnamon into a saucepan, pour in 1 litre/1¾ pints of the stock and bring to the boil. Reduce the heat, cover and simmer for 30 minutes.

2. Meanwhile, scrub the clams under cold running water and remove any with broken shells or that do not shut immediately when sharply tapped. Put them into a saucepan, pour in the wine, cover and cook over a high heat, shaking the pan occasionally, for 3–5 minutes, until the clams have opened. Remove from the heat and lift out the clams with a slotted spoon, reserving the cooking liquid. Discard any clams that remain shut and remove the remainder from the half shells. Strain the cooking liquid through a fine strainer into a bowl.

3. Remove the pan of fish and vegetables from the heat and leave to cool slightly, then ladle the mixture into a food processor or blender, in batches if necessary, and process until smooth.

4. Return the soup to the pan, add the remaining stock and the reserved cooking liquid and bring back to the boil. Reduce the heat and gradually stir in the cream; do not allow the soup to come back to the boil. Add the clams, season to taste with salt and pepper and simmer, stirring frequently, for 2 minutes, until heated through. Drizzle with olive oil, garnish with parsley and serve immediately.

Serves 6

350 g/12 oz white fish fillet, skinned

250 g/9 oz sweet potato, diced

1 onion, chopped

2 carrots, diced

½ tsp ground cinnamon

1.7 litres/3 pints basic vegetable stock

400 g/14 oz live clams

150 ml/5 fl oz dry white wine

225 ml/8 fl oz single cream

salt and pepper

extra virgin olive oil, for drizzling

chopped fresh parsley, to garnish

20

Clam & Pasta Soup

1. Heat the oil in a large saucepan. Add the onion and garlic and cook over a low heat, stirring occasionally, for 5 minutes, until softened. Add the tomatoes, tomato purée, sugar, oregano and stock and season with salt and pepper. Mix well and bring to the boil, then reduce the heat, cover and simmer, stirring occasionally, for 10 minutes.

2. Meanwhile, scrub the clams under cold running water and discard any with broken shells or that do not shut immediately when sharply tapped. Put the clams into a saucepan, pour in the wine, cover and cook over a high heat, shaking the pan occasionally, for 3–5 minutes, until the clams have opened. Remove from the heat and lift out the clams with a slotted spoon, reserving the cooking liquid. Discard any clams that remain shut and remove the remainder from the half shells. Strain the reserved cooking liquid through a fine strainer into a bowl.

3. Add the pasta to the soup and simmer, uncovered, for 10 minutes. Add the clams and the reserved cooking liquid, stir well and heat gently for 4–5 minutes; do not allow the soup to come back to the boil. If the soup is very thick, add a little hot water or stock. Taste and adjust the seasoning, if necessary, stir in the parsley and serve immediately.

Serves 6

- 3 tbsp olive oil
- 1 Spanish onion, finely chopped
- 3 garlic cloves, finely chopped
- 600 g/1 lb 5 oz canned chopped tomatoes
- 2 tbsp tomato purée
- 2 tsp sugar
- 1 tsp dried oregano
- 1 litre/1¾ pints basic vegetable stock
- 500 g/1 lb 2 oz live clams
- 175 ml/6 fl oz dry white wine
- 85 g/3 oz conchigliette or other small pasta shapes
- 3 tbsp chopped fresh flat-leaf parsley
- salt and pepper

Quick Scallop Soup with Pasta

1. Slice the scallops in half horizontally and season with salt and pepper.

2. Pour the milk and stock into a saucepan, add a pinch of salt and bring to the boil. Add the petit pois and pasta, bring back to the boil and cook for 8–10 minutes, until the taglialini is tender but still firm to the bite.

3. Meanwhile, melt the butter in a frying pan. Add the spring onions and cook over a low heat, stirring occasionally, for 3 minutes. Add the scallops and cook for 45 seconds on each side. Pour in the wine, add the prosciutto and cook for 2–3 minutes.

4. Stir the scallop mixture into the soup, taste and adjust the seasoning, if necessary, and garnish with the parsley. Serve immediately.

Serves 6

500 g/1 lb 2 oz shelled scallops

350 ml/12 fl oz milk

1.5 litres/2¾ pints basic vegetable stock

250 g/9 oz frozen petits pois

175 g/6 oz taglialini

70 g/2½ oz butter

2 spring onions, finely chopped

175 ml/6 fl oz dry white wine

3 slices of prosciutto, cut into thin strips

salt and pepper

chopped fresh parsley, to garnish

Mediterranean Fish Soup with Garlic Mayonnaise

1. Cut out and discard the gills of any reserved fish heads. Cut the fish fillets into chunks. Put the fish bones, heads and trimmings into a saucepan, pour in the wine vinegar, half the lemon juice and the stock, add the herbes de Provence and bay leaves and bring to the boil. Season with salt, reduce the heat and simmer for 30 minutes.

2. Meanwhile, make the garlic mayonnaise. Pound the garlic with the salt in a mortar with a pestle. Transfer to a bowl, add the egg yolks and whisk briefly with an electric mixer until creamy. Mix together the oils in a jug and, whisking constantly, gradually add them to the egg mixture. When about half the oil has been incorporated, add the remainder in a thin, steady stream, whisking constantly. Stir in lemon juice to thin to the desired consistency. Transfer the mayonnaise to a sauce boat, cover and set aside.

3. Strain the cooking liquid into a bowl, measure, and make up to 1.7 litres/3 pints with water, if necessary. Return to the saucepan.

4. Beat the egg yolks with the remaining lemon juice in a bowl and stir it into the pan. Add the pieces of fish, stir gently to mix and cook over a low heat for 7–8 minutes. Do not allow the soup to boil. Remove from the heat and serve in warmed soup bowls with toasted bread.

Serves 6

2 kg/4 lb 8 oz mixed white fish, such as gurnard, red mullet, snapper, grouper and haddock, filleted, with bones, heads and trimmings reserved

2 tbsp white wine vinegar

2 tbsp lemon juice

1.7 litres/3 pints basic vegetable stock

2 tsp herbes de Provence

2 bay leaves

4 egg yolks

salt

toasted country bread, to serve

Garlic mayonnaise
4 garlic cloves

pinch of salt

2 egg yolks

125 ml/4 fl oz extra virgin olive oil

125 ml/4 fl oz sunflower or safflower oil

1–2 tbsp lemon juice

Tasty

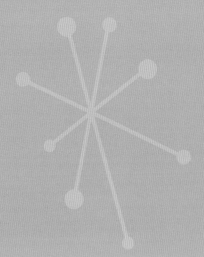

23

Carrot & Parsnip Soup

1. Put the carrots, parsnips, shallots and chervil into a saucepan, pour in the stock and season with salt and pepper. Bring to the boil, reduce the heat and simmer for 20–25 minutes, until the vegetables are tender.

2. Remove the pan from the heat and leave to cool slightly. Remove and discard the chervil, then transfer to a food processor or blender, in batches if necessary, and process to a purée.

3. Return the soup to the rinsed-out pan and reheat gently. Ladle into warmed bowls, swirl about 1 tablespoon of cream on the top of each and serve.

Serves 6

350 g/12 oz carrots, chopped

350 g/12 oz parsnips, chopped

4 shallots, chopped

4 fresh chervil sprigs

850 ml/1½ pints basic vegetable stock

salt and pepper

double cream, to garnish

24

Carrot & Coriander Soup

1. Heat the oil in a large saucepan. Add the onion and cook over a low heat, stirring occasionally, for 5 minutes, until softened.

2. Add the potato and celery and cook, stirring occasionally, for a further 5 minutes, then add the carrots and cook, stirring occasionally, for 5 minutes more. Cover the pan, reduce the heat to very low and cook, shaking the pan occasionally, for 10 minutes.

3. Pour in the stock and bring to the boil, then cover and simmer for 10 minutes, until the vegetables are tender.

4. Meanwhile, melt the butter in a frying pan. Add the coriander seeds and cook, stirring constantly, for 1 minute. Add the chopped coriander and cook, stirring constantly, for 1 minute, then remove from the heat.

5. Remove the soup from the heat and leave to cool slightly. Transfer to a food processor or blender, in batches if necessary, and process to a purée. Return the soup to the rinsed-out pan, stir in the coriander mixture and milk and season to taste with salt and pepper. Reheat gently, then serve, sprinkled with chopped coriander.

Serves 6

3 tbsp olive oil

1 red onion, chopped

1 large potato, chopped

1 celery stick, chopped

500 g/1 lb 2 oz carrots, chopped

1 litre/1¾ pints basic vegetable stock

1 tbsp butter

2 tsp coriander seeds, crushed

1½ tbsp chopped fresh coriander, plus extra to garnish

225 ml/8 fl oz milk

salt and pepper

Cream of Tomato Soup

1. Melt the butter in a large saucepan. Add the onion and cook over a low heat, stirring occasionally, for 5 minutes, until softened. Add the tomatoes, bay leaf, basil and parsley, season with salt and pepper and simmer, stirring occasionally, for 15 minutes, until the tomatoes have cooked down and most of the liquid has evaporated.

2. Increase the heat to medium, pour in the stock and bring to the boil. Reduce the heat, cover and simmer for 25 minutes.

3. Meanwhile, make the croûtons. Cut the bread into 5-mm/ ¼-inch squares. Heat the oil in a frying pan. Add the bread squares and cook, turning and tossing frequently, until golden brown all over. Remove with a slotted spoon and drain on kitchen paper.

4. Remove the soup from the heat and leave to cool slightly. Remove and discard the herbs and stir the tomato ketchup into the soup. Transfer the soup to a food processor or blender, in batches if necessary, and process to a purée. If any tomato seeds remain, pass the purée through a fine sieve.

5. Return the soup to the rinsed-out pan and reheat. Stir in the cream and heat gently for 1–2 minutes more, until the soup is hot. Taste and adjust the seasoning, if necessary, and ladle into warmed bowls. Tear the basil leaves and sprinkle them over the soup, add the croûtons and serve immediately.

Serves 6

55 g/2 oz butter
1 onion, chopped
1 kg/2 lb 4 oz ripe tomatoes, peeled, seeded and chopped
1 bay leaf
4 fresh basil sprigs
4 fresh parsley sprigs
1.7 litres/3 pints basic vegetable stock
1 tbsp tomato ketchup
175 ml/6 fl oz double cream
salt and pepper
fresh basil leaves, to garnish

Croûtons
55 g/2 oz day-old bread, crusts removed
2 tbsp olive oil

Tomato & Parsnip Soup

1. Melt the butter in a saucepan. Add the onions and garlic and cook over a low heat, stirring occasionally, for 5 minutes, until softened. Add the parsnips and cook, stirring occasionally, for a further 5 minutes.

2. Sprinkle in the flour and thyme, season with salt and pepper and cook, stirring constantly, for 2 minutes. Remove the pan from the heat. Gradually stir in the stock, a little at a time, then stir in the milk and add the bay leaf and tomatoes.

3. Return the pan to medium heat and bring to the boil, stirring constantly. Reduce the heat, cover and simmer for 45 minutes, until the parsnips are tender.

4. Remove the pan from the heat and leave to cool slightly. Remove and discard the bay leaf. Transfer the soup to a food processor or blender, in batches if necessary, and process to a purée.

5. Return the soup to the rinsed-out pan and reheat gently, stirring occasionally. Taste and adjust the seasoning, if necessary. Ladle into warmed bowls, garnish with snipped chives and serve immediately.

Serves 6

25 g/1 oz butter

2 onions, chopped

1 garlic clove, finely chopped

500 g/1 lb 2 oz parsnips, chopped

3 tbsp plain flour

½ tsp dried thyme

1 litre/1¾ pints basic vegetable stock

150 ml/5 fl oz milk

1 bay leaf

400 g/14 oz canned chopped tomatoes

salt and pepper

snipped fresh chives, to garnish

27

Mushroom Soup

1. Tear the bread into pieces and put it into a bowl. Pour in cold water to cover and leave to soak for 10 minutes, then drain and squeeze out.

2. Meanwhile, melt the butter in a large saucepan. Add the onion and cook over a low heat, stirring occasionally, for 8–10 minutes, until golden. Add the mushrooms and garlic and cook, stirring frequently, for 5–7 minutes, until they have released their liquid.

3. Add the bread and thyme and pour in the wine. Cook for 2 minutes, until the alcohol has evaporated, then pour in the stock and bring to the boil over a medium heat. Reduce the heat, cover and simmer for 20–25 minutes.

4. Remove the pan from the heat and leave to cool slightly. Transfer the soup to a food processor or blender, in batches if necessary, and process to a purée.

5. Return the soup to the rinsed-out pan, season to taste with salt and pepper and reheat gently, stirring occasionally. Ladle into warmed bowls and serve.

Serves 6

140 g/5 oz ciabatta or other country bread, crusts removed

55 g/2 oz butter

1 small onion, chopped

650 g/1 lb 7 oz field mushrooms, roughly chopped

1 garlic clove, finely chopped

½ tsp dried thyme

150 ml/5 fl oz red wine or Madeira

1 litre/1¾ pints basic vegetable stock

salt and pepper

Mushroom & Ginger Soup

1. Heat the oil in a saucepan. Add the shallots and ginger and cook over a low heat, stirring occasionally, for 5 minutes, until softened. Add the mushrooms and cook, stirring frequently, for 5–7 minutes, until they have released their liquid.

2. Pour in the stock and bring to the boil. Reduce the heat and simmer for 10 minutes.

3. Remove the pan from the heat and leave to cool slightly. Transfer the soup to a food processor or blender, in batches if necessary, and process to a purée.

4. Return to the rinsed-out pan, stir in the soured cream, season to taste with salt and pepper and reheat gently, stirring occasionally. Ladle into warmed bowls, sprinkle with the parsley and serve immediately.

Serves 6

3 tbsp olive oil

4 shallots, chopped

2.5-cm/1-inch piece of fresh ginger, finely chopped

1 kg/2 lb 4 oz chestnut mushrooms, roughly chopped

1 litre/1¾ pints basic vegetable stock

150 ml/5 fl oz soured cream

salt and pepper

2 tbsp chopped fresh flat-leaf parsley, to garnish

Red Pepper Soup

1. Preheat the grill. Put the peppers on a baking sheet and grill, turning frequently, for 10 minutes, until blistered and charred. Remove with tongs, put them into a plastic bag, seal the top and leave until cool enough to handle. Peel, halve and deseed them, then chop the flesh.

2. Meanwhile, pour the stock into a saucepan and bring to the boil. Add the peppers, onion, carrots, cucumber and cauliflower and bring back to the boil. Reduce the heat, cover and simmer for 20 minutes.

3. Remove the pan from the heat and leave to cool slightly. Transfer the soup to a food processor or blender, in batches if necessary, and process to a purée.

4. Return the soup to the rinsed-out pan. Beat together the egg yolk and cream in a bowl and stir into the soup, season to taste with salt and pepper and reheat gently, stirring occasionally, but do not allow the soup to boil. Stir in the sherry, ladle into warmed bowls and serve immediately.

Serves 6

2 red peppers

1.3 litres/2¼ pints basic vegetable stock

1 Spanish onion, finely chopped

2 carrots, chopped

85 g/3 oz cucumber, peeled, deseeded and chopped

85 g/3 oz cauliflower florets

1 large egg yolk

6 tbsp double cream

3 tbsp dry sherry

salt and pepper

30

Cauliflower & Coconut Soup

1. Pour the stock into a saucepan and add the lemon grass, lime rind and galangal. Pound 1 garlic clove with the coriander roots in a mortar with a pestle and add to the pan. Bring to the boil, then reduce the heat, cover and simmer for 40 minutes. Meanwhile, finely chop the remaining garlic.

2. Remove the pan from the heat and strain the stock into a bowl. Discard the contents of the strainer.

3. Heat the oil in a saucepan. Add the spring onions, chillies and chopped garlic and cook over a low heat, stirring occasionally, for 5 minutes. Add the cauliflower and cook, stirring frequently, for 6–8 minutes, until just beginning to colour.

4. Add the strained stock, coconut milk, Thai fish sauce, if using, and chopped coriander and bring to the boil over a medium heat. Stir well, reduce the heat, cover and simmer for 25–30 minutes. Season to taste with salt and pepper and stir in the lime juice. Ladle into warmed bowls, garnish with browned onions and serve immediately.

Serves 6

- 1.3 litres/2¼ pints basic vegetable stock
- 2 lemon grass stalks, bruised
- coarsely grated rind of 1 lime
- 6 slices of galangal or fresh ginger
- 2 garlic cloves
- 6 coriander roots
- 3 tbsp groundnut oil
- 6 spring onions, thinly sliced
- 1 green chilli, deseeded and chopped
- 1 red bird's eye chilli, deseeded and thinly sliced
- 1 large cauliflower, cut into small florets
- 400 ml/14 fl oz canned coconut milk
- 2 tbsp Thai fish sauce (optional)
- 2 tbsp chopped fresh coriander
- 1 tbsp lime juice
- salt and pepper
- browned onions, to garnish (see page 19)

Jerusalem Artichoke Soup

1. Fill a bowl with water and stir in the lemon juice. Peel the artichokes and cut into chunks, then immediately drop them into the bowl of acidulated water to prevent discoloration.

2. Heat the butter with the oil in a large saucepan. Add the onion and cook over a low heat, stirring occasionally, for 5 minutes, until softened. Drain the artichokes, add them to the pan and stir well. Cover and cook, stirring occasionally, for 15 minutes.

3. Pour in the stock and milk, increase the heat to medium and bring to the boil. Reduce the heat, re-cover the pan and simmer for 20 minutes, until the artichokes are soft.

4. Remove the pan from the heat and leave to cool slightly. Add the chives and transfer the soup to a food processor or blender, in batches if necessary, and process to a purée.

5. Pour the soup back into the rinsed-out pan, stir in the cream and season with salt and pepper. Reheat gently, stirring occasionally, but do not allow the soup to boil. Ladle into warmed bowls, drizzle with olive oil and serve immediately with croûtons.

Serves 6

1 tbsp lemon juice

700 g/1 lb 9 oz Jerusalem artichokes

55 g/2 oz butter

1 tbsp sunflower oil

1 large onion, chopped

1.3 litres/2¼ pints basic vegetable stock

175 ml/6 fl oz milk

1 tbsp snipped fresh chives

100 ml/3½ fl oz double cream

salt and pepper

extra virgin olive oil, for drizzling

croûtons, to serve (see page 65)

Goulash Soup

1. Heat the oil in a large saucepan. Add the onion, garlic and carrots and cook over a low heat, stirring occasionally, for 8–10 minutes, until lightly coloured. Add the cabbage and red pepper and cook, stirring frequently, for 3–4 minutes.

2. Sprinkle in the flour and paprika and cook, stirring constantly, for 1 minute. Gradually stir in the stock, a little at a time. Increase the heat to medium and bring to the boil, stirring constantly. Season with salt, reduce the heat, cover and simmer for 30 minutes.

3. Add the potatoes and bring back to the boil, then reduce the heat, re-cover the pan and simmer for a further 20–30 minutes, until the potatoes are soft but not falling apart.

4. Taste and adjust the seasoning and add the sugar, if using. Ladle the soup into warmed bowls, swirl a little crème fraîche on top of each and serve immediately.

Serves 6

2 tbsp olive oil

1 large onion, chopped

2 garlic cloves, finely chopped

3–4 carrots, thinly sliced

½ Savoy cabbage, cored and shredded

1 small red pepper, deseeded and chopped

1 tbsp plain flour

2 tbsp sweet paprika

1 litre/1¾ pints basic vegetable stock

2 potatoes, cut into chunks

1–2 tsp sugar (optional)

salt and pepper

crème fraîche, to garnish

Bacon & Pumpkin Soup

1. Heat the oil in a large saucepan. Add the onions and cook over a low heat, stirring occasionally, for 5 minutes, until softened.

2. Add the pumpkin, bacon and nutmeg, stir well, then cover and simmer, stirring occasionally, for 5–8 minutes.

3. Pour in the stock, increase the heat to medium and bring to the boil. Reduce the heat and simmer for 10–15 minutes.

4. Meanwhile, make the bacon croûtons. Heat the oil in a frying pan. Add the bacon and fry for 4–6 minutes on each side, until crisp and all the fat has been released. Meanwhile, cut the bread into 1-cm/½-inch squares. Remove the bacon from the pan and drain on kitchen paper. Add the bread squares and cook, turning and tossing until golden brown all over. Remove from the pan and drain on kitchen paper.

5. Remove the pan from the heat and leave to cool slightly. Transfer the soup to a food processor or blender, in batches if necessary, and process to a purée. Return to the rinsed-out pan, season to taste with salt and pepper and re-heat gently, stirring occasionally.

6. Remove the soup from the heat and ladle into warmed bowls. Sprinkle with the croûtons, crumble the bacon over the top and serve immediately.

Serves 6

2 tbsp olive oil

2 onions, chopped

600 g/1 lb 5 oz canned unsweetened pumpkin

200 g/7 oz smoked bacon, diced

pinch of grated nutmeg

1.2 litres/2 pints basic vegetable stock

salt and pepper

Bacon croûtons

2 tbsp sunflower oil

4 rashers of smoked bacon

55 g/2 oz day-old bread, crusts removed

Lentil Soup with Ham

1. Heat the oil in a large saucepan. Add the onion, garlic, celery, carrot and potato and cook over a low heat, stirring occasionally, for 5–7 minutes, until softened. Add the ham and cook, stirring occasionally, for a further 3 minutes. Remove from the pan with a slotted spoon and set aside.

2. Add the lentils, stock, bay leaf and parsley sprigs to the pan, increase the heat to medium and bring to the boil. Reduce the heat and simmer, stirring occasionally, for 30 minutes.

3. Add the tomatoes and return the vegetables and ham to the pan. Stir well and simmer for 25–30 minutes more.

4. Remove and discard the bay leaf and parsley. Stir in the paprika and vinegar, season to taste with salt and pepper and heat through for 2–3 minutes. Ladle into warmed soup bowls and serve immediately.

Serves 6

3 tbsp olive oil

1 Spanish onion, chopped

3 garlic cloves, chopped

2 celery sticks, chopped

1 carrot, chopped

1 potato, chopped

175 g/6 oz smoked ham, chopped

450 g/1 lb green or brown lentils

3 litres/5¼ pints basic vegetable stock

1 bay leaf

4 fresh parsley sprigs

4 tomatoes, peeled and chopped

1½ tsp sweet paprika

4 tbsp sherry vinegar

salt and pepper

Scotch Broth

1. Put the lamb into a large saucepan, pour in the stock and bring to the boil over a medium–low heat, skimming off the scum that rises to the surface.

2. Add the onion, barley, peas and thyme sprig and bring back to the boil. Reduce the heat, cover and simmer for 1 hour.

3. Increase the heat to medium, add the leeks, swede, carrots and cabbage, season with salt and pepper and bring back to the boil. Stir, reduce the heat, cover and simmer for 30 minutes, until the meat and vegetables are tender.

4. Skim off any fat from the surface of the soup and taste and adjust the seasoning, if necessary. Ladle into warmed bowls, sprinkle with parsley and serve immediately.

Serves 6

1 kg/2 lb 4 oz boneless lamb, cut into cubes

* 1.7 litres/3 pints basic vegetable stock

1 onion, chopped

55 g/2 oz pearl barley

85 g/3 oz dried green peas, soaked overnight in water to cover and drained

1 fresh thyme sprig

2 leeks, chopped

1 swede or turnip, chopped

2 carrots, chopped

½ Savoy cabbage, cored and shredded

salt and pepper

2 tbsp chopped fresh parsley, to garnish

36

Lamb & Aubergine Soup

1. Preheat the oven to 200°C/400°F/Gas Mark 6. Prick the aubergines in several places with a fork and put them on a baking sheet. Bake, turning once or twice, for 50–60 minutes, until soft, then remove from the oven and leave to cool.

2. Meanwhile, heat the oil in a large saucepan. Add the lamb and cook over a medium heat, turning frequently, for 8–10 minutes, until lightly browned all over. Add the stock and onion and bring to the boil. Reduce the heat and simmer for 1½ hours.

3. Remove the lamb from the pan with a slotted spoon and leave to cool slightly. Add the potatoes, cinnamon, coriander and cumin to the pan, stir well and bring back to the boil. Reduce the heat and simmer for 20–25 minutes, until the potatoes have softened.

4. Meanwhile, cut the meat off the bones and chop into bite-sized pieces. Peel the aubergines and roughly chop the flesh.

5. Remove the pan from the heat and leave to cool slightly. Remove and discard the cinnamon stick. Ladle the soup into a food processor or blender, in batches if necessary, add the aubergines and process to a purée.

6. Return the purée to the rinsed-out pan, add the lamb and parsley, season to taste with salt and pepper and reheat gently, stirring occasionally. Garnish with lemon slices and serve with rye bread.

Serves 6

2 aubergines

2 tbsp olive oil

1.8 kg/4 lb lamb shanks or scrag end and middle neck of lamb

2.5 litres/4½ pints basic vegetable stock

1 large onion, chopped

2 potatoes, cut into chunks

1 cinnamon stick

½ tsp ground coriander

½ tsp ground cumin

3 tbsp chopped fresh parsley

salt and pepper

lemon slices, halved, to garnish

rye bread, to serve

37

Lamb & Lemon Soup

1. Put the flour into a plastic bag and season with salt and pepper. Add the cubes of lamb, a few at a time, seal the bag and shake to coat. Shake off any excess.

2. Heat the oil in a large saucepan. Add the lamb and cook over a medium heat, stirring frequently, for 8–10 minutes, until lightly browned all over. Pour in the stock and bring to the boil, skimming off the scum that rises to the surface.

3. Add the carrots, onions and cayenne pepper, season with salt and pepper and bring back to the boil. Reduce the heat, cover and simmer for 1½–2 hours, until the meat is tender.

4. Meanwhile, make the garnish. Melt the butter in a saucepan over a very low heat or in a microwave-safe bowl in the microwave. Remove from the heat and stir in the cinnamon and paprika.

5. Beat the egg yolks with the lemon juice in a bowl. Remove the pan from the heat and whisk a ladleful of the hot soup into the egg mixture, then add it to the pan. Return the pan to a very low heat and heat through, gently rotating the pan, for 1–2 minutes; do not allow the soup to boil.

6. Ladle the soup into a warm tureen, spoon the spiced melted butter over the top, sprinkle with the mint and serve immediately, accompanied by flatbread.

Serves 6

55 g/2 oz plain flour

500 g/1 lb 2 oz boneless leg of lamb, cut into cubes

3 tbsp olive oil

1.2 litres/2 pints basic vegetable stock

2 carrots, cut into chunks

2 onions, cut into quarters

1 tsp cayenne pepper

3 egg yolks

2 tbsp lemon juice

salt and pepper

3 tbsp chopped fresh mint, to garnish

flatbread, to serve

To garnish
55 g/2 oz butter

½ tsp ground cinnamon

2 tsp sweet or hot paprika

Cream of Chicken Soup

1. Put the chicken into a large saucepan, pour in the stock, add the bouquet garni and season with salt and pepper. Bring to the boil over a medium heat, skimming off the scum that rises to the surface. Reduce the heat, cover and simmer for 1–1¼ hours, until the chicken is tender.

2. Remove the chicken from the pan and leave to cool. Strain the stock into a bowl and leave to cool, then either chill in the refrigerator overnight or in the freezer for 30 minutes.

3. Meanwhile, mash the butter into the flour in a small bowl to make a paste.

4. Remove and discard the chicken skin, cut the meat off the bones and roughly chop. Remove any fat that has solidified on the surface of the stock. Put the chicken and stock into a food processor or blender, in batches if necessary, and process to a smooth purée.

5. Transfer the purée to the rinsed-out pan and heat gently. Gradually whisk in the butter and flour mixture, in small pieces at a time, making sure each piece has been fully incorporated before adding the next. Bring to the boil, stirring constantly, then reduce the heat and simmer for 5 minutes. Taste and adjust the seasoning, if necessary, and stir in the cream. Serve immediately, garnished with croûtons.

Serves 6

1 chicken, about 1.3 kg/3 lb

1.5 litres/2¾ pints basic vegetable stock

1 bouquet garni (3 fresh parsley sprigs, 2 fresh thyme sprigs, 1 fresh tarragon sprig and 1 bay leaf tied together)

1 tbsp butter, softened

2 tbsp plain flour

4 tbsp double cream

salt and pepper

croûtons, to garnish (see page 65)

Cream of Clam Soup

1. Melt the butter in a saucepan. Add the onion and garlic and cook over a low heat, stirring occasionally, for 5 minutes, until softened.

2. Stir in the flour and cook, stirring constantly, for 1 minute, then remove the pan from the heat. Gradually stir in the stock, a little at a time, then stir in the wine.

3. Return the pan to medium heat, add the bay leaf and parsley sprigs, season with salt and pepper and bring to the boil, stirring constantly. Reduce the heat, cover and simmer for 15 minutes.

4. Meanwhile, drain the clams, reserving the juices. Finely chop the clams.

5. Add the clams and the reserved juices to the pan, bring back to the boil and simmer for a further 5 minutes.

6. Remove and discard the bay leaf and parsley sprigs. Gradually stir in the cream and heat through gently, but do not allow the soup to boil. Taste and adjust the seasoning, if necessary, and ladle into warmed bowls. Sprinkle with the chopped parsley and serve immediately with wholemeal bread.

Serves 6

40 g/1½ oz butter

1 large onion, finely chopped

2 garlic cloves, finely chopped

1 tbsp plain flour

400 ml/14 fl oz basic vegetable stock

125 ml/4 fl oz medium-dry white wine

1 bay leaf

6 fresh parsley sprigs

650 g/1 lb 7 oz bottled or canned clams

250 ml/9 fl oz single cream

salt and pepper

3 tbsp chopped fresh parsley, to garnish

wholemeal bread, to serve

Cajun Crab & Sweetcorn Chowder

1. Melt the butter in a large saucepan. Add the onion, garlic, celery and carrot and cook over a low heat, stirring occasionally, for 5 minutes, until softened.

2. Increase the heat to medium, pour in the wine and cook for 2 minutes, until the alcohol has evaporated. Pour in the stock and bring to the boil, then add the sweetcorn kernels, cayenne pepper and mixed herbs. Bring back to the boil, reduce the heat and simmer for 15 minutes.

3. Add the cream and simmer gently over a very low heat for a further 10–15 minutes, but do not allow the soup to boil.

4. Gradually add the crème fraîche, whisking constantly with a balloon whisk, then stir in the dill and crab meat and season to taste with salt and pepper. Heat gently for 3–4 minutes, then serve with wholemeal bread rolls.

Serves 6

40 g/1½ oz butter
1 onion, finely chopped
2 garlic cloves, finely chopped
2 celery sticks, finely chopped
1 small carrot, finely chopped
175 ml/6 fl oz medium-dry white wine
500 ml/18 fl oz basic vegetable stock
250 g/9 oz frozen sweetcorn kernels
pinch of cayenne pepper
½ tsp dried mixed herbs
350 ml/12 fl oz double cream
175 ml/6 fl oz crème fraîche
1 tbsp chopped fresh dill
225 g/8 oz white crab meat
salt and pepper
wholemeal bread rolls, to serve

Fish & Sweetcorn Soup

1. Put the fish fillets into a heatproof dish that will fit into a steamer and sprinkle with the wine. Put the slices of ginger in a garlic crusher and squeeze out the juice over the fish. You may have to do this in batches. Leave to marinate for 15 minutes.

2. Pour the stock into a saucepan and bring to the boil. Put the dish of fish into the steamer and set it over the saucepan. Cover and steam for 8–10 minutes, until the flesh flakes easily. Remove the steamer and set the dish of fish aside.

3. Add the sweetcorn to the stock and bring back to the boil, then stir in the sesame oil and season with salt. Reduce the heat and simmer for 10 minutes.

4. Meanwhile, mash the fish fillets with a fork. Mix the cornflour to a paste with the water.

5. Add the cornflour paste to the soup and cook, stirring constantly, until thickened. Add the fish and cook for 2–3 minutes, or until heated through.

6. Taste and adjust the seasoning, if necessary, then ladle into warmed bowls. Sprinkle with the spring onions and serve immediately.

Serves 6

650 g/1 lb 7 oz sea bass or sea bream fillets, skinned

2 tsp Chinese rice wine or dry sherry

2-cm/¾-inch piece of fresh ginger, thinly sliced

1.3 litres/2¼ pints basic vegetable stock

350 g/12 oz frozen sweetcorn kernels

1 tsp sesame oil

2½ tsp cornflour

3 tbsp water

salt and pepper

2 spring onions, chopped, to garnish

42

Carrot & Mussel Soup

1. Reserve 3 carrots and slice the remainder. Melt 55 g/2 oz of the butter in a large saucepan. Add the sliced carrots and half the sugar and cook over a low heat, stirring occasionally, for 5 minutes. Increase the heat to medium, pour in the stock, season with salt and bring to the boil. Reduce the heat, cover and simmer, stirring occasionally, for 25 minutes. Meanwhile, finely chop the reserved carrots. Melt the remaining butter in a small saucepan. Add the carrots and the remaining sugar and cook over a low heat, stirring occasionally, for 10 minutes, then remove from the heat.

2. Scrub the mussels under cold running water and pull off the 'beards'. Discard any with broken shells or that do not shut immediately when sharply tapped. Put them into a saucepan, pour in the wine and add the garlic. Cover and cook over a high heat, shaking the pan occasionally, for 4–5 minutes, until they open. Remove the pan from the heat and lift out the mussels. Discard any that remain shut. Remove the mussels from the half shell. Strain the cooking liquid through a muslin-lined strainer into a bowl. Remove the saucepan of stock and sliced carrots from the heat and leave to cool slightly, then ladle into a food processor or blender, add the cooking liquid and process to a purée. Return the soup to the rinsed-out pan, season to taste and reheat gently.

3. Gently stir in the mussels along with the carrot and sugar mixture, sprinkle with parsley and serve with wholemeal rolls.

Serves 6

1 kg/2 lb 4 oz carrots

100 g/3½ oz butter

1 tsp sugar

1.3 litres/2¼ pints basic vegetable stock

48 live mussels

300 ml/10 fl oz dry white wine

1 garlic clove, roughly chopped

salt and pepper

2 tbsp chopped fresh parsley, to garnish

wholemeal bread rolls, to serve

Stylish

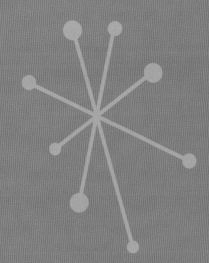

43

Asparagus Soup with Caviar

1. Trim off and reserve the woody ends of the asparagus, leaving the spears 7–8 cm/2¾–3½ inches long. Pour the stock into a saucepan, add the woody asparagus ends and bring to the boil. Reduce the heat and simmer for 15 minutes. Meanwhile, cut the remaining asparagus into 2.5-cm/1-inch lengths.

2. Bring a saucepan of lightly salted water to the boil. Add half the asparagus tips and simmer for 7–10 minutes, until tender. Remove from the heat, drain and reserve. Remove the stock from the heat and strain into a bowl. Discard the woody asparagus ends.

3. Melt 40 g/1½ oz of the butter in a large saucepan, add the leeks and remaining asparagus and cook over a low heat, stirring occasionally, for 5 minutes. Pour in the stock, season with salt and pepper and bring to the boil over a medium heat. Reduce the heat, cover and simmer for 10–15 minutes, until the asparagus is tender. Remove the pan from the heat and leave to cool slightly. Ladle the soup into a food processor or blender, in batches if necessary, and process to a purée.

4. Melt the remaining butter in a saucepan. Stir in the flour and cook, stirring constantly, for 1 minute. Stir in the purée and bring to the boil, stirring constantly. Add the milk and cook, stirring, for a few minutes more, then stir in the cream and reserved asparagus tips. Ladle the soup into warmed bowls, top each with a teaspoonful of caviar and serve immediately.

Serves 6

500 g/1 lb 2 oz asparagus spears

1 litre/1¾ pints basic vegetable stock

70 g/2½ oz butter

175 g/6 oz leeks, thinly sliced

25 g/1 oz plain flour

150 ml/5 fl oz milk

6 tbsp double cream

salt and pepper

6 tsp caviar or keta (salmon roe), to garnish

44

Avocado Soup

1. Halve the avocados lengthways and gently twist the halves apart. Remove and discard the stones and scoop out the flesh. Chop into small pieces, put them into a bowl, sprinkle with the lemon juice and toss well to coat. Melt the butter in a saucepan. Add the shallots and cook over a low heat, stirring occasionally, for 5 minutes, until softened. Stir in the flour and cook, stirring constantly, for 1 minute. Remove the pan from the heat and gradually stir in the stock. Return the pan to medium heat and bring to the boil, stirring constantly. Add the avocados, reduce the heat, cover and simmer for 15 minutes.

2. Meanwhile, preheat the grill to make the guacamole croûtes. Toast the bread on one side under the grill. Turn the slices over, brush with the oil and toast the second side. Remove from the heat. Scoop out the avocado flesh into a bowl and mash with the lime juice and chilli, to taste, and season. Divide the avocado mixture among the croûtes and set aside.

3. Remove the soup from the heat and push it through a strainer set over a bowl. Return the soup to the rinsed-out pan, stir in the cream, season to taste with salt and pepper and reheat gently, but do not allow the soup to boil.

4. Ladle the soup into warmed bowls, drizzle with olive oil and garnish with the lime slices. Serve with the croûtes.

Serves 6

3 ripe avocados

2 tbsp lemon juice

85 g/3 oz butter

6 shallots, chopped

1½ tbsp plain flour

850 ml/1½ pints basic vegetable stock

175 ml/6 fl oz single cream

salt and pepper

extra virgin olive oil, for drizzling

1 lime, thinly sliced, to garnish

Guacamole croûtes

6 thin slices of day-old baguette

olive oil, for brushing

½ large ripe avocado, stoned and brushed with lime juice

juice of 1 lime

¼–½ tsp chilli or Tabasco sauce

45

Broccoli & Stilton Soup

1. Melt the butter in a large saucepan. Add the onions and potato and stir well. Cover and cook over a low heat for 7 minutes. Add the broccoli and stir well, then re-cover the pan and cook for a further 5 minutes.

2. Increase the heat to medium, pour in the stock and bring to the boil. Reduce the heat, season with salt and pepper, re-cover and simmer for 15–20 minutes, until the vegetables are tender.

3. Remove the pan from the heat, strain into a bowl, reserving the vegetables, and leave to cool slightly. Put the vegetables into a food processor or blender, add 1 ladleful of the stock and process to a smooth purée. With the motor running, gradually add the remaining stock.

4. Return the soup to the rinsed-out pan and reheat gently, but do not allow the soup to boil. Remove from the heat and stir in the cheese until melted and thoroughly combined. Stir in the mace and taste and adjust the seasoning, if necessary. Ladle into warmed bowls, sprinkle with the croûtons and serve immediately.

Serves 6

40 g/1½ oz butter

2 white onions, chopped

1 large potato, chopped

750 g/1 lb 10 oz broccoli, cut into small florets

1.5 litres/2¾ pints basic vegetable stock

150 g/5½ oz Stilton cheese, diced

pinch of ground mace

salt and pepper

croûtons, to garnish (see page 65)

46

Spicy Cucumber Soup

1. Pour the stock into a saucepan, add the lemon grass, 2 tablespoons of the lime juice and the coriander sprigs and bring to the boil over a medium heat. Reduce the heat, cover and simmer for 25 minutes.

2. Remove the pan from the heat and strain the stock into a clean pan. Stir in the remaining lime juice and the cucumber and season to taste with salt and pepper.

3. Bring back to the boil, stirring constantly, then reduce the heat and simmer for 5 minutes.

4. Remove the pan from the heat, taste and adjust the seasoning, if necessary, and ladle into warmed bowls. Divide the spring onions, chillies and coriander among the bowls and serve immediately.

Serves 6

* 1.2 litres/2 pints basic vegetable stock
2 tbsp chopped lemon grass
3½ tbsp lime juice
16 fresh coriander sprigs
175 g/6 oz cucumber, peeled and cut into julienne strips
salt and pepper

To garnish
3 spring onions, thinly sliced
3 green chillies, deseeded and finely chopped
2 tbsp chopped fresh coriander

47

Vegetable Broth

1. Pour the stock into a saucepan and bring to the boil over a medium heat. Add the corn cobs and carrots and cook for 3 minutes, then add the mangetout, mushrooms and Chinese leaves and cook for a further 2 minutes.

2. Add the Chinese chives and soy sauce and season to taste with salt, if necessary (soy sauce is very salty), and pepper. Simmer for 2–3 minutes more, then ladle into warmed bowls, garnish with the spring onions and serve immediately.

Serves 6

* 1 litre/1¾ pints basic vegetable stock
85 g/3 oz baby corn cobs, thinly sliced diagonally
85 g/3 oz baby carrots, thinly sliced diagonally
85 g/3 oz mangetout or French beans, sliced diagonally
85 g/3 oz chestnut mushrooms, thinly sliced
85 g/3 oz Chinese leaves or spinach, shredded
1 tbsp chopped Chinese chives
2 tbsp light soy sauce
salt and pepper
thinly sliced spring onions, to garnish

48

Vegetable Soup with Semolina Dumplings

1. First, make the dumplings. Pour the milk into a saucepan and add the water, sugar, nutmeg and salt. Bring to the boil over a medium heat, then reduce the heat and sprinkle the semolina over the surface of the liquid. Simmer, stirring constantly, until thickened, then remove the pan from the heat and leave to cool for 15 minutes. Stir in the beaten egg until thoroughly combined, then cover and chill in the refrigerator for 30 minutes.

2. To make the soup, blanch the turnips and carrots in a pan of boiling water for 3 minutes, then drain. Melt the butter in a large saucepan, add the turnips and carrots and cook over a low heat, stirring frequently, for 5 minutes.

3. Sprinkle the sugar over the vegetables, increase the heat to medium and cook, stirring constantly, until they begin to caramelize. Pour in the stock, season with salt and pepper and bring to the boil, then reduce the heat and simmer for 20 minutes.

4. Meanwhile, flour your hands and shape the semolina mixture into small balls. About 7–10 minutes before the end of the cooking time, add the dumplings to the soup and simmer until they have risen to the surface.

5. Taste and adjust the seasoning, if necessary, and ladle the soup into warmed bowls. Sprinkle with the parsley and serve immediately.

Serves 6

55 g/2 oz turnips, diced

175 g/6 oz carrots, diced

55 g/2 oz butter

1½ tsp sugar

1.7 litres/3 pints basic vegetable stock

salt and pepper

3 tbsp chopped fresh parsley, to garnish

Dumplings

5 tbsp milk

150 ml/5 fl oz water

1 tsp sugar

pinch of grated nutmeg

pinch of salt

125 g/4½ oz semolina

1 large egg, lightly beaten

plain flour, for dusting

49

Curried Vegetable Soup

1. Melt the butter in a large saucepan. Add the onions and garlic and cook over a low heat, stirring occasionally, for 8–10 minutes, until lightly browned. Stir in the cumin and coriander and cook, stirring constantly, for 2 minutes. Add the sweet potato, carrots and parsnips and cook, stirring frequently, for 5 minutes, then stir in the curry paste and mix well. Increase the heat to medium, pour in the stock and bring to the boil, stirring occasionally. Reduce the heat, cover and simmer for 20–25 minutes, until the vegetables are tender.

2. Meanwhile, make the garnish. Cut the ginger in half and then into thin julienne strips. Heat the oil in a small frying pan over a high heat. Reduce the heat, add the ginger and cook, stirring and turning constantly, for 1 minute. Remove with a slotted spoon and drain on kitchen paper.

3. Remove the pan of soup from the heat and leave to cool slightly. Ladle the soup into a food processor or blender, in batches if necessary, and process to a purée.

4. Return the soup to the rinsed-out pan and stir in the milk. Cook, stirring occasionally, for 5 minutes. Stir in the lime juice and 3 tablespoons of the soured cream and season to taste with salt and pepper.

5. Ladle the soup into warmed bowls, add a swirl of the remaining soured cream and garnish with the fried ginger. Serve immediately with naan bread.

Serves 6

40 g/1½ oz butter

2 onions, chopped

2 garlic cloves, finely chopped

1½ tsp ground cumin

1 tsp ground coriander

1 sweet potato, chopped

2 carrots, chopped

3 parsnips, chopped

1 tbsp curry paste

700 ml/1¼ pints basic vegetable stock

700 ml/1¼ pints milk

1 tsp lime juice

6 tbsp soured cream

salt and pepper

naan bread, to serve

To garnish
10-cm/4-inch piece of fresh ginger

2 tbsp groundnut oil

50

Mexican Tomato & Vermicelli Soup

1. Put the onion, garlic, chillies and tomatoes into a food processor or blender and process to a smooth purée.

2. Heat the oil in a heavy-based frying pan. Add the vermicelli and stir-fry over a low heat, until golden brown. Remove from the pan and drain on kitchen paper.

3. Add the vegetable purée to the frying pan and cook, stirring constantly, for 6–8 minutes, until thickened. Remove the pan from the heat.

4. Spoon the vegetable purée into a large saucepan, pour in the stock, stir in the tomato ketchup and tomato purée and add the vermicelli and coriander. Season to taste with salt and pepper and bring to the boil. Reduce the heat, cover and simmer for 5 minutes, or until the vermicelli is tender.

5. Ladle the soup into warmed bowls, sprinkle with the shreds of lime rind and serve immediately.

Serves 6

1 Spanish onion, chopped

2 garlic cloves, chopped

1–2 red Serrano chillies, deseeded and chopped

650 g/1 lb 7 oz tomatoes, peeled, deseeded and chopped

3 tbsp corn oil

85 g/3 oz vermicelli

1.5 litres/2¾ pints basic vegetable stock

1 tbsp tomato ketchup

1 tbsp tomato purée

1 tbsp chopped fresh coriander

salt and pepper

finely shredded lime rind, to garnish

Clear Shiitake Mushroom Soup with Egg

1. Pour the stock into a saucepan, add the kombu and bring just to the boil over a low heat. Immediately remove the kombu. Add the bonito flakes and bring to the boil, then remove the pan from the heat and leave the bonito flakes to settle. Strain the stock through a muslin-lined sieve into a clean pan.

2. Meanwhile, cut off and discard the mushroom stems and thinly slice the caps.

3. Bring the stock to the boil. Reduce the heat, add the mushrooms and simmer for 2–3 minutes, until just tender but still firm to the bite. Stir in the Japanese soy sauce and sake and season to taste with salt.

4. Increase the heat to medium–low. Gradually pour in the eggs, moving the bowl round and round the saucepan so that they are evenly distributed and so set immediately. Simmer for about 15 seconds, then remove the pan from the heat.

5. Break up the 'omelette' and divide it and the soup among warmed bowls. Garnish with the spring onions and serve immediately.

Serves 6

- 850 ml/1½ pints basic vegetable stock
- 10 g/¼ oz kombu seaweed
- 10 g/¼ oz bonito flakes
- 6 shiitake mushrooms
- 1 tbsp Japanese soy sauce
- 2 tsp sake or dry white wine
- 2 large eggs, lightly beaten
- salt
- thinly sliced spring onions, to garnish

Egg Flower Soup

1. Pour the stock into a saucepan and stir in the rice wine, soy sauce and sesame oil. Put the slices of ginger into a garlic crusher and squeeze out the juice into the saucepan. Add the Chinese leaves and bring to the boil, then reduce the heat and simmer for 3–4 minutes.

2. Increase the heat to medium–low. Gradually pour the eggs into the centre of the soup in a steady stream. Simmer for 2 seconds, then stir to break the eggs into filaments. Season to taste, ladle into warmed bowls and serve immediately.

Serves 6

* 1 litre/1¾ pints basic vegetable stock

3 tbsp Chinese rice wine or dry sherry

3 tbsp light soy sauce

1 tsp sesame oil

1-cm/½-inch piece fresh ginger, thinly sliced

6 Chinese leaves or pak choi, shredded

2 eggs, beaten

salt and pepper

53

Garlic Soup

1. Crush the garlic cloves with the flat side of a heavy knife blade, then peel off and discard the skins. Put the garlic cloves into a saucepan and add the bay leaf, cloves, peppercorns, saffron, parsley sprigs, chervil sprigs, thyme sprigs, sage leaves and olive oil.

2. Pour in the stock and bring to the boil, then reduce the heat, cover and simmer for 40 minutes.

3. Remove the pan from the heat and strain the soup into a warmed tureen. Season to taste with salt and pepper, sprinkle with the parsley and serve with wholemeal bread rolls and sprinkled with grated Parmesan cheese.

Serves 6

2 garlic bulbs, separated into cloves

1 bay leaf

3 cloves

3 black peppercorns

½ tsp saffron threads

2 fresh flat-leaf parsley sprigs

2 fresh chervil sprigs

4 fresh thyme sprigs

16 fresh sage leaves

1½ tbsp olive oil

1.7 litres/3 pints basic vegetable stock

salt and pepper

2 tbsp chopped fresh flat-leaf parsley, to garnish

To serve
wholemeal bread rolls
grated Parmesan cheese

Hot & Sour Soup

1. Pour the stock into a saucepan and add the lime leaves, lemon grass, half the chillies, half the spring onions and the garlic. Bring to the boil, then reduce the heat and simmer for 30 minutes.

2. Remove the pan from the heat and strain the soup into a clean pan. Discard the contents of the strainer.

3. Return the soup to the heat, stir in the lime juice, sugar, coriander, remaining chillies and remaining spring onions and season to taste with salt. Bring back to the boil, then reduce the heat and simmer for 5 minutes. Add the tofu and carrots and simmer for a further 4–5 minutes. Serve immediately.

Serves 6

- 1.3 litres/2¼ pints basic vegetable stock
- 6 fresh or dried kaffir lime leaves
- 3 lemon grass stalks, cut into 4-cm/1½-inch lengths
- 3 fresh red chillies, deseeded and sliced
- 6 spring onions, thinly sliced
- 3 garlic cloves, thinly sliced
- 6 tbsp lime juice
- 2 tsp sugar
- 2 tbsp chopped fresh coriander
- 350 g/12 oz firm tofu, thinly sliced
- 2 carrots, thinly sliced
- salt

Pork Rib Soup with Pickled Mustard Leaves

1. Heat the oil in a small frying pan or wok. Add the garlic and stir-fry for a few minutes, until golden. Transfer to a plate and set aside.

2. Pour the stock into a saucepan and bring to the boil over a medium heat. Add the spare ribs and bring back to the boil, then reduce the heat, cover and simmer for 15 minutes, until tender.

3. Meanwhile, put the cellophane noodles into a bowl, pour in hot water to cover and leave to soak for 10 minutes, until softened. Drain well.

4. Add the noodles and pickled leaves to the soup and bring back to the boil. Stir in the Thai fish sauce and sugar, season to taste with pepper and ladle into warmed bowls. Garnish with the garlic slices and red and green chillies and serve immediately.

Serves 6

1 tbsp groundnut oil

3 garlic cloves, thinly sliced

1.2 litres/2 pints basic vegetable stock

500 g/1 lb 2 oz pork spare ribs

85 g/2 oz cellophane noodles

280 g/10 oz canned Thai pickled mustard leaves or Chinese snow pickles, well-rinsed and roughly chopped

2 tbsp Thai fish sauce

½ tsp sugar

pepper

1 red and 1 green chilli, deseeded and thinly sliced, to garnish

56

Chicken Noodle Soup

1. Bring a saucepan of water to the boil. Add the noodles and cook according to the instructions on the packet. Drain, refresh under cold running water and leave to stand in a bowl of water.

2. Heat the oil in a large saucepan. Add the spring onions and bacon and cook over a low heat, stirring occasionally, for 5 minutes, until the spring onions have softened and the bacon is beginning to colour.

3. Add the tarragon and chicken, increase the heat to medium and cook, stirring frequently, for about 8 minutes, until the chicken is golden brown all over.

4. Pour in the wine and cook for 2 minutes, until the alcohol has evaporated, then pour enough of the stock just to cover the meat. Reduce the heat, cover and simmer for 20–30 minutes, until the chicken is tender.

5. Pour in the remaining stock, season with salt and pepper and bring to the boil. Add the noodles and heat through briefly. Ladle the soup into warmed bowls and serve immediately, with crusty bread and sprinkled with Parmesan cheese.

Serves 6

175 g/6 oz egg noodles

2 tbsp olive oil

8 spring onions, chopped

4 bacon rashers, chopped

2 tsp chopped fresh tarragon

6 skinless boneless chicken thighs, diced

150 ml/5 fl oz dry white wine

1.2 litres/2 pints basic vegetable stock

salt and pepper

To serve
grated Parmesan cheese
crusty bread

Crab & Noodle Soup

1. Bring a saucepan of water to the boil. Add the noodles and cook according to the instructions on the packet. Drain, refresh under cold running water and leave to stand in a bowl of water.

2. Heat the oil in a large saucepan. Add the shallots, carrots and celery and cook over a low heat, stirring occasionally, for 5 minutes, until softened.

3. Increase the heat to medium, pour in the vermouth and cook for 2 minutes, until the alcohol has evaporated. Pour in the stock and bring to the boil, then reduce the heat and simmer for 10 minutes.

4. Meanwhile, flake the crab meat and remove any pieces of shell or cartilage. Drain the noodles and add them to the pan. Add the crab and stir in the anchovy essence and lemon juice. Season to taste with salt and pepper. Simmer for a few minutes more to heat through, then ladle the soup into warmed bowls, garnish with the chopped parsley and serve immediately.

Serves 6

150 g/5½ oz egg noodles

3 tbsp groundnut oil

4 shallots, chopped

2 carrots, chopped

2 celery sticks, chopped

6 tbsp dry vermouth

1.7 litres/3 pints basic vegetable stock

175 g/6 oz white crab meat, thawed if frozen

a few drops of anchovy essence

1 tbsp lemon juice

salt and pepper

chopped fresh parsley, to garnish

Prawn Bisque

1. Melt the butter in a large saucepan. Add the onion, carrots, celery and bay leaves and cook over a low heat, stirring occasionally, for 8–10 minutes, until golden brown. Increase the heat to medium, add the prawns and cook, stirring occasionally, for 4–5 minutes, until they change colour.

2. Pour in the brandy and wine and cook for a further 4–5 minutes, until the alcohol has evaporated and the prawns are cooked. Remove the prawns and leave to cool slightly.

3. Add the tomatoes, tomato purée, parsley and stock to the pan and bring to the boil, reduce the heat and simmer for 30 minutes. Meanwhile, peel the prawns, discarding the shells. Devein the prawns by cutting a slit along their backs with a sharp knife and removing the black vein with the point of the knife. Chop the prawns.

4. Remove the soup from the heat, add the chopped prawns and leave to cool slightly. Ladle the soup into a food processor or blender, in batches if necessary, and process to a purée. Pour the soup through a strainer into the rinsed-out pan, pressing the contents of the strainer with the back of a ladle to extract as much liquid as possible. Bring the soup back to the boil, then reduce the heat and stir in the cream, lemon juice and cayenne pepper. Taste and adjust the seasoning, if necessary, and heat for 1–2 minutes more, but do not allow the soup to boil. Ladle into warmed bowls, drizzle over the cream and add some cayenne pepper to garnish.

Serves 6

85 g/3 oz butter

1 small onion, chopped

2 small carrots, chopped

1 celery stick, chopped

2 bay leaves

650 g/1 lb 7 oz unshelled raw prawns

3 tbsp brandy

100 ml/3½ fl oz dry white wine

650 g/1 lb 7 oz tomatoes, chopped

1½ tsp tomato purée

2 fresh parsley sprigs

✳ 2.5 litres/4½ pints basic vegetable stock

6 tbsp double cream, plus extra to decorate

1 tbsp lemon juice

pinch of cayenne pepper or dash of Tabasco sauce, plus extra, to garnish

salt and pepper

Cool

59

Al Fresco Avocado Soup

1. Halve the avocados lengthways and gently twist the halves apart. Remove and discard the stones and, using a teaspoon, scoop out the flesh.

2. Put the avocado flesh, lemon juice, stock, shallot and chilli and garlic sauce into a food processor or blender and process to a smooth purée. Scrape into a bowl and whisk in the cream with a balloon whisk. Season to taste with salt and pepper.

3. Cover tightly with clingfilm and chill in the refrigerator for at least 3 hours. To serve, stir the soup and taste and adjust the seasoning, if necessary. Ladle into individual bowls, garnish with watercress sprigs and serve immediately.

Serves 6

2 avocados

1 tbsp lemon juice

✳ 1 litre/1¾ pints basic vegetable stock

1 shallot, chopped

dash of chilli and garlic sauce

150 ml/5 fl oz double cream

salt and pepper

watercress sprigs, to garnish

60

Broad Bean Soup

1. Pour the stock into a saucepan and bring to the boil. Reduce the heat to a simmer, add the beans and cook for about 7 minutes, until just tender.

2. Remove the pan from the heat and leave to cool slightly. Ladle into a food processor or blender, in batches if necessary, and process to a purée. Strain the purée into a bowl to remove the skins.

3. Stir in the lemon juice and summer savoury and season to taste with salt and pepper. Leave to cool completely, then cover with clingfilm and chill in the refrigerator for at least 3 hours.

4. To serve, stir the soup and taste and adjust the seasoning, if necessary. Ladle into bowls and garnish with the yogurt and fresh mint leaves.

Serves 6

* 850 ml/1½ pints basic vegetable stock

650 g/1 lb 7 oz shelled young broad beans

3 tbsp lemon juice

2 tbsp chopped fresh summer savoury

salt and pepper

To garnish

6 tbsp Greek-style yogurt, chilled

fresh mint leaves or marjoram flowers

Cucumber & Mint Soup

1. Pour the stock into a large saucepan, add the spring onions and bring to the boil. Reduce the heat and simmer for 10 minutes. Reserve a little of the diced cucumber for the garnish and add the remainder and the mint sprigs to the pan. Simmer for a further 20 minutes. Remove the pan from the heat and leave to cool slightly.

2. Remove and discard the mint sprigs. Ladle the soup into a food processor or blender, in batches if necessary, and process to a purée. Return the soup to the rinsed-out pan and reheat gently, but do not allow the soup to boil.

3. Mix the cornflour to a paste with the water in a bowl. Stir the paste into the saucepan and bring to the boil, stirring constantly. Simmer, stirring constantly, for a few minutes, until thickened.

4. Stir in the cream and season to taste with salt and pepper. Remove the pan from the heat and stir in a few drops of food colouring, if using, to give the soup an attractive pale green colour. Leave to cool completely, then cover with clingfilm and chill in the refrigerator for at least 3 hours.

5. To serve, ladle into bowls, garnish with the reserved cucumber and fresh mint leaves and drizzle over the oil. Serve with warm pitta bread.

Serves 6

* 1.3 litres/2¼ pints basic vegetable stock
6 spring onions, chopped
2 cucumbers, peeled, deseeded and diced
3 fresh mint sprigs
1½ tbsp cornflour
3 tbsp water
5 tbsp double cream
green food colouring (optional)
salt and pepper
fresh mint leaves, to garnish
extra virgin olive oil, for drizzling
warm pitta bread, to serve

Curried Cucumber Soup

1. Whisk together the crème fraîche, 225 ml/8 fl oz of the yogurt, the curry powder and cayenne pepper in a bowl until thoroughly combined.

2. Stir in the onion, cucumbers, coriander and stock and season to taste with salt and pepper. Cover with clingfilm and chill in the refrigerator for at least 3 hours. Chill the remaining yogurt.

3. To serve, stir the soup and taste and adjust the seasoning, if necessary. Ladle into bowls, garnish with the remaining yogurt and fresh coriander sprigs and serve with garlic naan bread.

Serves 6

125 ml/4 fl oz crème fraîche

350 ml/12 fl oz natural yogurt

1–1½ tsp curry powder

pinch of cayenne pepper

1 white onion, grated

2 cucumbers, peeled, deseeded and diced

4 tbsp finely chopped fresh coriander

300 ml/10 fl oz basic vegetable stock

salt and pepper

fresh coriander sprigs, to garnish

garlic naan bread, to serve

63

Pea Soup

1. Pour the stock into a saucepan, add the onion and garlic and bring to the boil over a medium heat. Reduce the heat and simmer for 15 minutes.

2. Increase the heat to medium, add the petits pois, mint, lavender, if using, and sugar and bring back to the boil. Reduce the heat and simmer for a further 5–7 minutes.

3. Remove the pan from the heat and leave to cool completely. Remove and discard the herb sprigs. Ladle the soup into a food processor or blender, in batches if necessary, and process to a smooth purée.

4. Transfer to a bowl and stir in the lemon juice and soured cream. Season to taste with salt and pepper, cover with clingfilm and chill in the refrigerator for at least 3 hours. To serve, stir well, taste and adjust the seasoning, if necessary, and ladle into bowls.

Serves 6

* 850 ml/1½ pints basic vegetable stock
1 Spanish onion, finely chopped
2 garlic cloves, finely chopped
350 g/12 oz frozen petits pois
2 fresh mint sprigs
1 fresh lavender sprig (optional)
½ tsp sugar
1 tbsp lemon juice
225 ml/8 fl oz soured cream or natural yogurt
salt and pepper

Asparagus Soup

1. Cut off the tips of the asparagus and set aside. Cut the remaining spears into 1-cm/½-inch lengths.

2. Melt the butter in a large saucepan. Add the spring onions and cook over a low heat, stirring occasionally, for 5 minutes. Add the pieces of asparagus spears and cook, stirring occasionally, for a further 5 minutes.

3. Stir in the flour and cook, stirring constantly, for 2 minutes. Remove the pan from the heat and gradually stir in the stock. Return the pan to medium heat and bring to the boil, stirring constantly. Reduce the heat, season with salt and pepper and simmer for 35–40 minutes.

4. Meanwhile, bring a pan of water to the boil. Add the asparagus tips and cook for 5–8 minutes, until tender. Drain and cut in half.

5. Remove the soup from the heat and leave to cool slightly. Ladle it into a food processor or blender, in batches if necessary, and process to a smooth purée. Pour the soup into a bowl and stir in the crème fraîche, lemon rind and asparagus tips. Leave to cool completely, then cover with clingfilm and chill in the refrigerator for at least 3 hours.

6. To serve, stir the soup and taste and adjust the seasoning, if necessary. Ladle into bowls, sprinkle with Parmesan cheese and serve with melba toast.

Serves 6

1 kg/2 lb 4 oz asparagus, trimmed

55 g/2 oz butter

6 spring onions, chopped

3 tbsp plain flour

1.4 litres/2½ pints basic vegetable stock

125 ml/4 fl oz crème fraîche

1 tsp finely grated lemon rind

salt and pepper

To serve
grated Parmesan cheese
melba toast

Carrot & Orange Soup

1. Melt the butter in a large saucepan. Add the shallots and carrots and cook over a low heat, stirring occasionally, for 5–8 minutes, until softened.

2. Pour in the stock, increase the heat to medium and bring to the boil. Season with salt and pepper, reduce the heat, cover and simmer for 1 hour.

3. Remove the pan from the heat and leave to cool slightly. Ladle the soup into a food processor or blender, in batches if necessary, and process to a smooth purée.

4. Transfer the soup to a bowl and stir in the orange juice and orange rind. Leave to cool completely, then cover with clingfilm and chill in the refrigerator for at least 3 hours.

5. To serve, stir in the cream, taste and adjust the seasoning, if necessary, ladle into bowls and garnish with carrot strips.

Serves 6

40 g/1½ oz butter

4 shallots, chopped

600 g/1 lb 5 oz baby carrots, sliced

✳ 1 litre/1¾ pints basic vegetable stock

350 ml/12 fl oz orange juice

grated rind of 1 orange

150 ml/5 fl oz single cream, chilled

salt and pepper

carrot strips, to garnish

66

Beetroot & Egg Soup

1. Put the beetroots and lemons into a large saucepan, pour in the stock and bring to the boil. Reduce the heat and simmer for 20 minutes.

2. Remove the pan from the heat and leave to cool slightly. Ladle the soup into a food processor or blender, in batches if necessary, and process to a purée. Pass the soup through a strainer into a bowl to remove any membrane or fibres. Leave to cool completely.

3. Meanwhile, put the eggs, honey and a pinch of salt into a food processor or blender and process until thoroughly combined. Gradually add the mixture to the soup, stirring constantly.

4. Cover with clingfilm and chill in the refrigerator for at least 3 hours. To serve, stir the soup and taste and adjust the seasoning, if necessary. Ladle into bowls, drizzle with honey, garnish with the sour cream and snipped chives and serve immediately.

Serves 6

650 g/1 lb 7 oz cooked beetroots, peeled and chopped

2 lemons, peeled, deseeded and chopped

1.3 litres/2¼ pints basic vegetable stock

3 large eggs

1½ tbsp clear honey, plus extra for drizzling

salt

To garnish
soured cream, chilled
snipped fresh chives

Vichyssoise

1. Melt the butter in a large saucepan. Add the leeks and onions and stir well. Cover and cook over a low heat, stirring occasionally, for 8–10 minutes, until very soft but not coloured.

2. Increase the heat to medium, add the potatoes, pour in the stock and bring to the boil. Reduce the heat, cover and simmer for 25 minutes. Stir in the cream, season with salt and pepper and cook for a further 5 minutes, but do not allow the soup to boil.

3. Remove the pan from the heat and leave to cool slightly. Ladle the soup into a food processor or blender, in batches if necessary, and process to a smooth purée.

4. Pour the soup into a bowl and leave to cool completely. Cover with clingfilm and chill in the refrigerator for at least 3 hours.

5. To serve, stir the soup and taste and adjust the seasoning, if necessary. Ladle into bowls, garnish with the snipped chives and serve immediately.

Serves 6

40 g/1½ oz butter

550 g/1 lb 4 oz leeks, finely chopped

1½ onions, chopped

225 g/8 oz potatoes, thickly sliced

1.3 litres/2¼ pints basic vegetable stock

350 ml/12 fl oz double cream

salt and pepper

snipped fresh chives, to garnish

Leek, Potato & Pear Soup

1. Measure 3 tablespoons of the stock into a small bowl, stir in the saffron and set aside.

2. Melt the butter in a large saucepan. Add the leeks and potatoes and cook over a low heat, stirring occasionally, for 5 minutes, until the leeks have softened.

3. Increase the heat to medium, add the pears, pour in the stock and the saffron mixture and bring to the boil, stirring frequently. Reduce the heat, cover and simmer for 20–25 minutes, until the vegetables and pears are tender.

4. Remove the pan from the heat and leave to cool slightly. Ladle the soup into a food processor or blender, in batches if necessary, and process to a smooth purée.

5. Pour the soup into a bowl, season to taste with salt and pepper and leave to cool completely. Cover with clingfilm and chill in the refrigerator for at least 3 hours.

6. To serve, stir the soup and taste and adjust the seasoning, if necessary. Ladle into bowls, top each with a spoonful of crème fraîche and a sprig of watercress and serve immediately.

Serves 6

* 1.3 litres/2¼ pints basic vegetable stock
pinch of saffron strands, lightly crushed
40 g/1½ oz butter
350 g/12 oz leeks, thinly sliced
175 g/6 oz potatoes, diced
3 ripe pears, peeled, cored and chopped
salt and pepper

To garnish
crème fraîche, chilled
watercress sprigs

69

Apple & Fennel Soup

1. Melt the butter in a large saucepan. Add the onion and garlic and cook over a low heat, stirring occasionally, for 5 minutes, until softened. Add the fennel and potatoes and cook, stirring occasionally, for a further 8–10 minutes.

2. Gradually pour in the cider, taking care as it will foam, and cook for 2 minutes, until the alcohol has evaporated. Increase the heat to medium, add the star anise, bouquet garni, lemon juice and stock and bring to the boil. Season to taste with salt and pepper, reduce the heat and simmer for 20–25 minutes, until the vegetables are tender.

3. Remove the pan from the heat and leave to cool slightly. Remove and discard the star anise and bouquet garni. Ladle the soup into a food processor or blender, in batches if necessary, and process to a smooth purée.

4. Transfer the soup to a bowl and leave to cool completely. Cover with clingfilm and chill in the refrigerator for at least 3 hours.

5. To serve, stir in the crème fraîche and taste and adjust the seasoning, if necessary. Ladle into bowls, garnish each with a lemon slice and fennel fronds and serve immediately.

Serves 6

25 g/1 oz butter

1 small onion, chopped

1 small garlic clove, finely chopped

1 large fennel bulb, fronds reserved, diced

2 potatoes, diced

300 ml/10 fl oz dry cider

1 star anise

1 bouquet garni (3 fresh parsley sprigs, 2 fresh thyme sprigs and 1 bay leaf, tied together)

2 tbsp lemon juice

✳ 600 ml/1 pint basic vegetable stock

225 ml/8 fl oz crème fraîche or Greek-style yogurt, chilled

salt and pepper

6 lemon slices, to garnish

Apple Soup

1. Reserve 2 of the apples and peel, core and dice the remainder. Put the diced apple into a bowl, add the lemon juice and toss well to prevent discoloration.

2. Melt 40 g/1½ oz of the butter in a large saucepan. Add the leeks and stir well, then cover and cook over a low heat, stirring occasionally, for 8–10 minutes, until softened.

3. Add the diced apple and cook, stirring occasionally, for a further 5 minutes. Add the potatoes and cook, stirring occasionally, for 5 minutes more. Increase the heat to medium, pour in the stock and bring to the boil. Reduce the heat, cover and simmer for 45–50 minutes, until the leeks and apples are very soft.

4. Remove the pan from the heat and leave to cool slightly. Ladle the soup into a food processor or blender, in batches if necessary, and process to a smooth purée. Transfer to a bowl, stir in the cream and nutmeg, season to taste with salt and pepper and leave to cool completely. Cover with clingfilm and chill for at least 3 hours.

5. To serve, peel, core and dice the reserved apples. Melt the remaining butter in a frying pan. Add the diced apples and cook over a low heat, stirring occasionally, for 5 minutes until lightly coloured and softened, but not disintegrating. Remove with a slotted spoon and drain on kitchen paper. Stir the soup and taste and adjust the seasoning, if necessary. Ladle into bowls, garnish with the fried apples and serve immediately.

Serves 6

1 kg /2 lb 4oz apples
2 tbsp lemon juice
70 g/2½ oz butter
2 leeks, sliced
2 potatoes, diced
✳ 1.4 litres/2½ pints basic vegetable stock
150 ml/5 fl oz double cream
pinch of grated nutmeg
salt and pepper

Roasted Red Pepper Soup with Garlic Croûtons

1. Preheat the grill. Put the peppers on a baking sheet and grill, turning frequently, for 10 minutes, until the skins are charred. Remove with tongs, put them into a plastic bag, tie the top and leave until cool enough to handle. Peel off the skins, halve and deseed, then roughly chop the flesh.

2. Heat the oil in a large saucepan. Add the onion and garlic and cook over a low heat, stirring occasionally, for 5 minutes, until softened. Add the peppers and tomatoes, stir well, cover and cook, stirring occasionally, for 8–10 minutes, until pulpy. Increase the heat to medium, pour in the wine and cook for 2 minutes, until the alcohol has evaporated. Stir in the sugar, pour in the stock and bring to the boil. Season with salt and pepper, reduce the heat and simmer for 30 minutes.

3. Remove the pan from the heat and leave to cool slightly. Ladle the soup into a food processor or blender and process to a purée. Transfer to a bowl and leave to cool completely, then cover with clingfilm and chill in the refrigerator for at least 3 hours.

4. To make the garlic croûtons, heat the oil in a frying pan. Add the garlic and stir-fry over a low heat for about 2 minutes. Remove and discard the garlic, add the diced bread and cook, stirring and tossing frequently, until golden brown all over.

5. Ladle the soup into bowls, drizzle with chilli oil, garnish with the garlic croûtons and serve immediately.

Serves 6

3 red peppers

3 tbsp olive oil

1 Spanish onion, chopped

3 garlic cloves, finely chopped

1 kg/2 lb 4 oz ripe tomatoes, peeled, deseeded and roughly chopped

6 tbsp red wine

1 tsp sugar

✳ 1 litre/1¾ pints basic vegetable stock

salt and pepper

chilli oil, for drizzling

Garlic croûtons

3 tbsp olive oil

2 garlic cloves, chopped

3 slices of day-old bread, crusts removed, cut into 5-mm/¼-inch dice

72

Quick-and-easy Chickpea Soup with Tahini

1. Heat a heavy-based frying pan. Add the coriander and cumin seeds and cook over a low heat, stirring constantly, for a few minutes, until they give off their aroma. Remove from the heat, tip the seeds into a mortar and pound with a pestle until ground.

2. Pour the stock into a food processor or blender, add the tahini, lemon juice, garlic and roasted spices and process until thoroughly combined. Pour into a bowl, stir in the mint and season to taste with salt and pepper. Cover with clingfilm and chill for 1 hour.

3. To serve, stir the soup and taste and adjust the seasoning, if necessary. Stir in the chickpeas, ladle into bowls, drizzle with olive oil and garnish with coriander. Serve immediately with warm pitta bread.

Serves 6

½ tsp coriander seeds

1 tsp cumin seeds

✳ 600 ml/1 pint basic vegetable stock

450 ml/16 fl oz tahini

350 ml/12 fl oz lemon juice

2 garlic cloves, finely chopped

1 tbsp chopped fresh mint

200 g/7 oz canned chickpeas, drained and rinsed

salt and pepper

extra virgin olive oil, for drizzling

chopped fresh coriander, to garnish

warm pitta bread, to serve

Jellied Vegetable Consommé

1. Heat the oil in a large saucepan. Add the onion and leek, stir well, cover and cook over a low heat, stirring occasionally, for 30 minutes. Add the tomatoes and mushrooms and cook for 5 minutes, then pour in the stock and bring to the boil. Cover and simmer for 1 hour.

2. Remove the pan from the heat, strain the stock into a bowl, pressing the vegetables with the back of a ladle to extract as much liquid as possible, stir in the yeast extract and leave to cool completely. Discard the contents of the strainer.

3. Return the cooled stock to a clean pan and whisk in the egg whites. Bring to the boil over a medium–low heat. When the egg whites float on the surface, reduce the heat and simmer for 1 minute. Remove from the heat and strain the stock through a muslin-lined strainer into a bowl. Leave to cool. Pour 150 ml/5 fl oz of the cooled stock into a saucepan, sprinkle the gelatine over the surface and leave for 5 minutes, until spongy. (If using vegetarian gelatine, follow the packet instructions.) Add 1.2 litres/2 pints of the remaining stock and simmer over a low heat, gently stirring occasionally, for 5 minutes, until the gelatine has dissolved completely. Remove the pan from the heat and leave to cool.

4. Stir the Madeira into the consommé and season to taste with salt and pepper. Pour into a bowl and chill in the refrigerator for 4 hours, until set. Chop the jellied consommé and spoon into individual bowls. Sprinkle with the parsley and serve immediately.

Serves 6

1 tbsp olive oil

1 small onion, finely chopped

1 leek, thinly sliced

2 tomatoes, halved crossways

225 g/8 oz chestnut mushrooms, sliced

1.5 litres/2¾ pints basic vegetable stock

2 tsp yeast extract

2 egg whites

1 sachet (15 g/½ oz) powdered gelatine

175 ml/6 fl oz Madeira or medium sherry

salt and pepper

chopped fresh parsley, to garnish

Cucumber & Prawn Soup

1. Pour the stock into a saucepan. Add the cucumber, spring onions and dill and bring to the boil. Reduce the heat and simmer for 20–25 minutes, until the vegetables are tender.

2. Remove the pan from the heat and leave to cool slightly. Ladle the soup into a food processor or blender, in batches if necessary, and process to a smooth purée.

3. Return the soup to the rinsed-out pan and reheat gently. Meanwhile, stir the cornflour to a paste with the water in a bowl. Stir the paste into the soup and bring to the boil, stirring constantly. Reduce the heat and simmer for 3 minutes, then remove from the heat, season to taste with salt and pepper, pour into a bowl and leave to cool completely.

4. Stir in a few drops of green food colouring, if using, and add the prawns. Cover with clingfilm and chill in the refrigerator for at least 3 hours.

5. Stir the soup and taste and adjust the seasoning, if necessary. Ladle into bowls, swirl in the cream and serve immediately.

Serves 6

- 1.3 litres/2¼ pints basic vegetable stock
- 2 cucumbers, peeled, halved lengthways, deseeded and sliced
- 10 spring onions, chopped
- 1 tbsp chopped fresh dill
- 5 tbsp cornflour
- 5 tbsp water
- green food colouring (optional)
- 85 g/3 oz peeled cooked prawns
- salt and pepper
- 6 tbsp single cream, chilled, to garnish

75

Tomato & Smoked Shellfish Soup

1. Pour the stock into a bowl. Add the tomatoes, cucumber, shallot, vinegar, sugar, mustard, Tabasco sauce and smoked shellfish and stir well. Season to taste with salt and pepper, cover with clingfilm and chill for at least 2 hours.

2. To serve, stir the soup and taste and adjust the seasoning, if necessary. Ladle into bowls, sprinkle with the croûtons and serve.

Serves 6

* 700 ml/1¼ pints basic vegetable stock
* 6 ripe tomatoes, peeled, deseeded and chopped
* 1 cucumber, peeled, halved lengthways, deseeded and chopped
* 1 shallot, chopped
* 3 tbsp sherry vinegar
* 1 tsp sugar
* 1½ tsp Dijon mustard
* ¼ tsp Tabasco sauce or pinch of cayenne pepper
* 500 g/1 lb 2 oz smoked oysters or smoked mussels
* salt and pepper
* croûtons, to serve (see page 65)

76

Mussel Soup

1. Scrub the mussels under cold running water and pull off the 'beards'. Discard any with broken shells or that do not shut immediately when sharply tapped. Put them into a large saucepan, pour in the stock and wine and add the onion, celery and parsley. Cover and bring to the boil over a high heat. Cook, shaking the pan occasionally, for 3–5 minutes, until the shells have opened.

2. Remove the pan from the heat and lift out the mussels with a slotted spoon. Discard any that remain shut, shell the remainder and set aside for another dish.

3. Strain the soup into a clean pan and discard the contents of the strainer. Stir in the cream and cayenne pepper, season to taste with salt and pepper and leave to cool completely. Cover with clingfilm and chill for at least 3 hours.

4. To serve, stir the soup and taste and adjust the seasoning, if necessary. Ladle into bowls and serve immediately with garlic and herb bread.

Serves 6

36 live mussels

150 ml/5 fl oz basic vegetable stock

300 ml/10 fl oz dry white wine

¼ onion, finely chopped

½ celery stick, finely chopped

5 tbsp chopped fresh flat-leaf parsley

600 ml/1 pint double cream

pinch of cayenne pepper or dash of Tabasco sauce

salt and pepper

garlic and herb bread, toasted, to serve

World Classics

77

Borscht–Russia

1. Peel and coarsely grate 4 of the beetroots. Melt the butter in a large saucepan. Add the onions and cook over a low heat, stirring occasionally, for 5 minutes, until softened. Add the grated beetroots, carrots and celery and cook, stirring occasionally, for a further 5 minutes.

2. Increase the heat to medium, add the tomatoes, vinegar, sugar, garlic and bouquet garni, season with salt and pepper and stir well, then pour in the stock and bring to the boil. Reduce the heat, cover and simmer for 1¼ hours.

3. Meanwhile, peel and grate the remaining beetroot. Add it and any juices to the pan and simmer for a further 10 minutes. Remove the pan from the heat and leave to stand for 10 minutes.

4. Remove and discard the bouquet garni. Ladle the soup into warmed bowls and top each with a spoonful of soured cream, sprinkle with chopped dill and serve immediately with rye bread.

Serves 6

5 raw beetroots, about 1 kg/2 lb 4 oz

70 g/2½ oz butter

2 onions, thinly sliced

3 carrots, thinly sliced

3 celery sticks, thinly sliced

6 tomatoes, peeled, deseeded and chopped

1 tbsp red wine vinegar

1 tbsp sugar

2 garlic cloves, finely chopped

1 bouquet garni (3 fresh parsley sprigs, 2 fresh thyme sprigs and 1 bay leaf, tied together)

1.3 litres/2¼ pints basic vegetable stock

salt and pepper

rye bread, to serve

To garnish
soured cream
chopped fresh dill

78

Onion Soup–France

1. Heat the oil with the butter in a large saucepan. Add the onions, stir well, cover and cook over a very low heat, stirring occasionally, for 15 minutes. Uncover the pan, increase the heat to medium, stir in the garlic, sugar, salt and cook, stirring frequently, for 30–40 minutes, until the onions are deep golden brown.

2. Meanwhile, bring the stock to the boil in another saucepan. Sprinkle the flour over the onions and cook, stirring constantly, for 3 minutes. Stir in the vermouth and cook, stirring constantly, for 2 minutes, until the alcohol has evaporated, then gradually stir in the hot stock and bring to the boil. Skim off any scum that rises to the surface, reduce the heat, cover and simmer for 40 minutes.

3. Meanwhile, preheat the grill. Toast the slices of bread on both sides. Rub each slice with the garlic clove, then top with the cheese and grill for a few minutes, until melted.

4. Stir in the brandy, remove the pan from the heat and taste and adjust the seasoning, if necessary. Ladle into warmed bowls, top each with a cheese croûte and serve immediately.

Serves 6

1 tbsp olive oil

25 g/1 oz butter

4–5 onions, about 650 g/
1 lb 7 oz, thinly sliced

3 garlic cloves, finely chopped

1 tsp sugar

1 tsp salt

2 litres/3½ pints basic
vegetable stock

2 tbsp plain flour

150 ml/5 fl oz dry white
vermouth

3 tbsp brandy

salt and pepper

Cheese croûtes
6 slices of French bread

1 garlic clove, halved

225 g/8 oz Gruyère cheese,
grated

Bouillabaisse—France

1. Cut the large fish into 3–4 pieces. Leave the small ones whole. Scrub the mussels under cold running water and pull off the 'beards'. Discard any with broken shells or that do not shut immediately when sharply tapped. Pour the stock into a saucepan and bring to the boil. Put the saffron into a bowl, pour in hot water to cover and leave to soak.

2. Put the onions, leeks, celery, fennel, tomatoes, garlic, orange rind, chilli, thyme sprig, bay leaves, peppercorns and cloves into a large saucepan. Put the firm-fleshed fish, such as monkfish, on top, pour in half the olive oil and season with salt. Pour in the stock, bring back to the boil, cover and simmer for 8 minutes.

3. Add the softer fish, the remaining olive oil and the saffron with its soaking water. Cover and simmer for a further 4 minutes. Add the mussels and langoustines, cover and cook for 4 minutes more, until the mussels have opened and all the fish is cooked. Discard any mussels that remain closed.

4. Carefully transfer the fish, shellfish and vegetables to a warmed serving dish. Strain the broth into a warmed tureen and taste and adjust the seasoning, if necessary. Serve the fish and broth immediately.

Serves 8

2.25 kg/5 lb mixed fish, such as monkfish, John Dory and red mullet

450 g/1 lb live mussels

3.4 litres/6 pints basic vegetable stock

½ tsp saffron threads

2 onions, chopped

2 leeks, white parts only, chopped

3 celery sticks, chopped

1 fennel bulb, sliced

2 large tomatoes, peeled and chopped

4 garlic cloves, finely chopped

1 strip of thinly pared orange rind

1 red chilli, deseeded and chopped

1 fresh thyme sprig

2 bay leaves

8 black peppercorns

2 cloves

225 ml /8 fl oz olive oil

450 g/1 lb cooked langoustines

salt and pepper

Bauernsuppe–Germany

1. Melt the butter in a large saucepan. Add the meat and cook over a medium heat, stirring frequently, for 8–10 minutes, until lightly browned all over. Meanwhile, bring the stock to the boil in another saucepan.

2. Add the onions to the meat, reduce the heat and cook, stirring frequently, for 5 minutes, until softened. Add the garlic and cook for 2 minutes more. Stir in the paprika and flour and cook, stirring constantly, for 3–4 minutes. Gradually stir in the hot stock and bring to the boil. Add the bouquet garni, season with salt, cover and simmer, stirring occasionally, for 1 hour.

3. Add the potatoes to the soup, re-cover the pan and simmer for a further 45 minutes, until the meat and vegetables are tender.

4. Remove the pan from the heat and taste and adjust the seasoning, if necessary. Remove and discard the bouquet garni. Ladle the soup into warmed bowls, sprinkle with the dill and grated cheese and serve immediately.

Serves 6

55 g/2 oz butter

1 kg/2 lb 4 oz stewing steak, trimmed of fat and cut into 2-cm/¾-inch cubes

2.5 litres/4½ pints basic vegetable stock

2 onions, chopped

1 garlic clove, finely chopped

1 tsp paprika

4 tbsp plain flour

1 bouquet garni (3 fresh parsley sprigs, 2 fresh thyme sprigs and 1 bay leaf, tied together)

3 potatoes, diced

salt and pepper

To garnish
2 tsp chopped fresh dill

55 g/2 oz Gruyère cheese, grated

81

Minestrone–Italy

1. Heat the oil in a large saucepan. Add the onion, garlic and celery and cook over a low heat, stirring occasionally, for 5–7 minutes, until the onion has softened. Stir in the cabbage and cook, stirring frequently, for a further 5 minutes.

2. Increase the heat to medium, pour in the wine and cook for about 2 minutes, until the alcohol has evaporated, then pour in the stock. Add the cannellini beans and bring to the boil, then lower the heat, cover and simmer for 2½ hours.

3. Add the tomatoes, tomato purée, sugar, carrots, peas, French beans, pasta and herbs and season to taste with salt and pepper. Simmer for 20–25 minutes, until the pasta is cooked and the vegetables are tender.

4. Ladle the soup into warm bowls and serve immediately, sprinkled with the Parmesan cheese.

Serves 6

2 tbsp olive oil

1 Spanish onion, chopped

2 garlic cloves, finely chopped

2 celery sticks, chopped

½ small white cabbage, cored and shredded

150 ml/5 fl oz red wine

1.7 litres/3 pints basic vegetable stock

55 g/2 oz dried cannellini beans, soaked overnight in cold water and drained

4 plum tomatoes, peeled, deseeded and chopped

2 tbsp tomato purée

2 tsp sugar

2 carrots, diced

55 g/2 oz fresh shelled peas

55 g/2 oz French beans, cut into short lengths

55g/2 oz ziti pasta

2 tbsp mixed herbs

salt and pepper

grated Parmesan cheese, to serve

Fabada–Spain

1. Bring the stock to the boil in a large saucepan. Add the beans, onion and garlic and bring back to the boil, then reduce the heat, cover and simmer for 1 hour, until the beans are tender.

2. Meanwhile, put the saffron into a small bowl, add water to cover and leave to soak.

3. Add the sausages, bacon, ham, thyme and saffron with its soaking water to the pan, season to taste with salt and pepper and mix well. Re-cover and simmer the soup for a further 30–35 minutes. Ladle into warmed bowls and serve immediately.

Serves 6

* 1.7 litres/3 pints basic vegetable stock
225 g/8 oz dried butter beans, soaked overnight in cold water to cover and drained
225 g/8 oz dried large white kidney beans (fabes de la granja) or cannellini beans, soaked overnight in water to cover and drained
1 Spanish onion, chopped
2 garlic cloves, finely chopped
pinch of saffron threads
125 g/4½ oz morcilla or other blood sausage, sliced
2 chorizo sausages, sliced
4 rashers of bacon, diced
55 g/2 oz smoked ham, diced
pinch of dried thyme
salt and pepper

Caldo Verde–Portugal

1. Heat 2 tablespoons of the olive oil in a large saucepan. Add the onion and garlic and cook over a low heat, stirring occasionally, for 5 minutes, until softened. Add the potatoes and cook, stirring constantly, for a further 3 minutes.

2. Increase the heat to medium, pour in the stock and bring to the boil. Reduce the heat, cover and cook for 10 minutes.

3. Meanwhile, heat the remaining olive oil in a frying pan. Add the sausage slices and cook over a low heat, turning occasionally, for a few minutes, until the fat runs. Remove with a slotted spoon and drain on kitchen paper.

4. Remove the pan of soup from the heat and mash the potatoes with a potato masher. Return to the heat, add the kale and bring back to the boil. Reduce the heat and simmer for 5–6 minutes, until tender.

5. Remove the pan from the heat and mash the potatoes again to incorporate. Stir in the sausage slices, season to taste with salt and pepper and ladle into warmed bowls. Drizzle each with a little olive oil and serve immediately.

Serves 6

3 tbsp olive oil, plus extra for drizzling

1 Spanish onion, finely chopped

2 garlic cloves, finely chopped

900 g/2 lb potatoes, diced

1.5 litres/2¾ pints basic vegetable stock

125 g/4½ oz chorizo or other spicy sausage, thinly sliced

450 g/1 lb kale or Savoy cabbage, finely shredded

salt and pepper

84

London Particular–England

1. Dice 6 rashers of the bacon. Melt the butter in a saucepan. Add the diced bacon and cook over a low heat, stirring frequently, for 4–5 minutes. Add the onions, carrots and celery and cook, stirring frequently, for a further 5 minutes.

2. Increase the heat to medium, add the peas, pour in the stock and bring to the boil. Reduce the heat, cover and simmer for 1 hour.

3. Meanwhile, preheat the grill. Grill the remaining bacon for 2–4 minutes on each side, until crisp, then remove from the heat. Leave to cool slightly, then crumble.

4. Remove the soup from the heat and season to taste with salt and pepper. Ladle into warmed bowls, garnish with the crumbled bacon and the croûtons and serve immediately.

Serves 6

8 thick rashers of bacon

25 g/1 oz butter

2 onions, chopped

2 carrots, chopped

2 celery sticks, chopped

125 g/4½ oz yellow split peas, soaked in cold water for 1–2 hours and drained

✳ 1.7 litres/3 pints basic vegetable stock

salt and pepper

croûtons, to garnish (see page 65)

85

Cullen Skink–Scotland

1. Put the fish, onion and parsley into a large saucepan, pour in the stock and bring to the boil, skimming off the scum that rises to the surface. Reduce the heat, cover and simmer for 10 minutes, until the flesh flakes easily.

2. Remove the pan from the heat and lift out the fish with a fish slice. Remove and discard the skin and bones and flake the flesh. Strain the stock into a clean pan.

3. Return the pan to the heat, add the potatoes and bring back to the boil. Reduce the heat and simmer for 20–30 minutes, until tender.

4. Remove the pan from the heat. Using a slotted spoon, transfer the potatoes to a bowl, add the butter and mash until smooth.

5. Return the pan to the heat, add the milk and bring to the boil. Whisk in the mashed potatoes, a little at a time, until thoroughly incorporated. Gently stir in the fish and season to taste with salt and pepper. Ladle into warmed bowls, sprinkle with chopped parsley and serve immediately with crusty bread.

Serves 6

500 g/1 lb 2 oz Finnan haddock or undyed smoked haddock

1 large onion, chopped

4 fresh parsley sprigs

1.3 litres/2¼ pints basic vegetable stock

750 g/1 lb 10 oz potatoes, cut into chunks

55 g/2 oz butter

850 ml/1½ pints milk

salt and pepper

chopped fresh parsley, to garnish

crusty bread, to serve

Mussel Soup—Ireland

1. Scrub the mussels under cold running water and pull off the 'beards'. Discard any with broken shells or that do not shut when sharply tapped. Sprinkle the onion, parsley and bay leaves over the base of a large saucepan, put the mussels on top, season, and pour in the cider. Cover, bring to the boil over a high heat and cook, shaking the pan occasionally, for 4–5 minutes, until the mussels have opened. Remove the pan from the heat and lift out the mussels. Discard any that remain shut. Remove the mussels from the shells and set aside. Strain the cooking liquid into a bowl.

2. Melt the butter in a saucepan. Add the celery and leeks and cook over a low heat, stirring occasionally, for 8 minutes, until lightly browned. Meanwhile, pour the milk into another saucepan and bring just to the boil, then remove from the heat.

3. Sprinkle the flour over the vegetables and cook, stirring constantly, for 2 minutes. Increase the heat and gradually stir in the milk, then stir in the stock. Bring to the boil, stirring constantly, then reduce the heat and simmer for 15 minutes.

4. Remove the pan from the heat and strain the soup into a bowl. Return to the rinsed-out pan, add the reserved cooking liquid, the nutmeg, fennel seeds and mussels. Stir in the cream and reheat gently but do not allow the soup to boil. Ladle into warmed bowls and serve with wholemeal bread.

Serves 6

48 live mussels
1 onion, finely chopped
2 tbsp chopped fresh parsley
2 bay leaves
250 ml/9 fl oz dry cider
55 g/2 oz butter
2 celery sticks, chopped
2 leeks, thinly sliced
600 ml/1 pint milk
40 g/1½ oz plain flour
600 ml/1 pint basic vegetable stock
pinch of grated nutmeg
½ tsp fennel seeds
225 ml/8 fl oz double cream
salt and pepper
wholemeal bread, to serve

87

Avgolemono–Greece

1. Pour the stock into a large saucepan and bring to the boil. Add the rice, bring back to the boil, then reduce the heat and simmer for 15 minutes, until the rice is tender.

2. Meanwhile, beat the eggs in a bowl and gradually beat in the lemon juice. Gradually beat in a ladleful of the hot soup, then add the mixture to the pan. Cook over a low heat, rotating the pan occasionally to distribute the egg and lemon sauce evenly, for 2–3 minutes.

3. Remove from the heat, season the soup to taste with pepper and ladle into warmed bowls. Sprinkle with parsley and serve immediately.

Serves 6

* 1.7 litres/3 pints basic vegetable stock
115 g/4 oz long-grain rice
4 eggs
125 ml/4 fl oz lemon juice
pepper
chopped fresh parsley, to garnish

Harira—North Africa

1. Heat the olive oil in a large saucepan. Add the lamb and cook over a medium heat, stirring frequently, for 8–10 minutes, until lightly browned all over. Reduce the heat, add the onion and cook, stirring frequently, for 5 minutes, until softened.

2. Increase the heat to medium, add the chickpeas, pour in the stock and bring to the boil. Reduce the heat, cover and simmer for 2 hours.

3. Stir in the lentils, tomatoes, red pepper, tomato purée, sugar, cinnamon, turmeric, ginger, coriander and parsley and simmer for a further 15 minutes. Add the rice and simmer for 15 minutes more, until the rice is cooked and the lentils are tender.

4. Season to taste with salt and pepper and remove the pan from the heat. Ladle the soup into warmed bowls, sprinkle with a little chopped coriander and serve immediately.

Serves 6

2 tbsp olive oil

225 g/8 oz boneless lean lamb, cut into cubes

1 onion, chopped

115 g/4 oz dried chickpeas, soaked overnight in water to cover and drained

1.5 litres/2¾ pints basic vegetable stock

115 g/4 oz red or yellow lentils

2 large tomatoes, peeled, deseeded and diced

1 red pepper, deseeded and diced

1 tbsp tomato purée

1 tsp sugar

1 tsp ground cinnamon

½ tsp ground turmeric

½ tsp ground ginger

1 tbsp chopped fresh coriander, plus extra to garnish

1 tbsp chopped fresh parsley

55 g/2 oz long-grain rice

salt and pepper

Eshkaneh–Iran

1. Melt the butter in a large saucepan. Add the onions and cook over a low heat, stirring occasionally, for 7–8 minutes, until just beginning to colour.

2. Sprinkle in the flour and cook, stirring constantly, for 2 minutes. Remove the pan from the heat and gradually stir in the stock, a little at a time. Return the pan to medium heat and bring to the boil, stirring constantly. Add the turmeric, lemon juice, sugar and coriander and season generously with salt and pepper. Reduce the heat, cover and simmer for 10 minutes.

3. Lightly beat the egg in a bowl. Whisk it into the soup and remove the pan from the heat. Ladle into warmed bowls and serve immediately with warmed flatbread.

Serves 6

55 g/2 oz butter

4 onions, thinly sliced

2 tbsp plain flour

✳ 1.2 litres/2 pints basic vegetable stock

1 tsp ground turmeric

125 ml/4 fl oz lemon juice

1 tbsp caster sugar

1 tbsp chopped fresh coriander

1 egg

salt and pepper

warmed flatbread, to serve

90

Wonton Soup–China

1. Mix together the pork, prawns, spring onion, ginger, sugar, rice wine and half the soy sauce in a bowl until thoroughly combined. Cover and leave to marinate for 20 minutes.

2. Put 1 teaspoon of the mixture in the centre of each wonton wrapper. Dampen the edges, fold corner to corner into a triangle and press to seal, then seal the bottom corners together.

3. Bring the stock to the boil in a large saucepan. Add the wontons and cook for 5 minutes. Stir in the remaining soy sauce and remove from the heat. Ladle the soup and wontons into warmed bowls, sprinkle with snipped chives and serve immediately.

Serves 6

175 g/6 oz minced pork or chicken

55 g/2 oz peeled prawns, minced

1 spring onion, finely chopped

1 tsp finely chopped fresh ginger

1 tsp sugar

1 tbsp Chinese rice wine or dry sherry

2 tbsp light soy sauce

24 ready-made wonton wrappers

✳ 850 ml/1½ pints basic vegetable stock

snipped fresh chives, to garnish

Three Delicacy Soup–China

1. Mix together the chicken and prawns in a bowl. Mix the cornflour to a paste with the water in another bowl and add to the mixture, together with the egg white and the salt, stirring well to coat.

2. Bring the stock to the boil in a saucepan over a medium heat. Add the chicken mixture and the ham and bring back to the boil. Reduce the heat and simmer for 1 minute. Taste and adjust the seasoning, if necessary, and remove from the heat. Ladle into warmed bowls, garnish with spring onions and serve immediately.

Serves 6

175 g/6 oz skinless, boneless chicken breast, very thinly sliced into strips

175 g/6 oz peeled raw prawns, halved if large

1 tsp cornflour

2 tsp water

1 small egg white, lightly beaten

pinch of salt

⁂ 1 litre/1¾ pints basic vegetable stock

175 g/6 oz honey-roast ham, very thinly sliced into strips

salt and pepper

chopped spring onions or snipped fresh chives, to garnish

Seaweed Soup with Miso-Japan

1. Heat the oil in a saucepan. Add the onion and garlic and cook over a low heat, stirring occasionally, for 5 minutes, until softened. Meanwhile, pour the stock into another saucepan and bring to the boil.

2. Stir the miso paste, tomato purée, ginger and coriander into the onion mixture, mixing well, then add the carrots and cook, stirring frequently, for 5 minutes. If the mixture looks as if it might scorch, stir in 1–2 tablespoons of the hot stock.

3. Add the yaki-nori to the stock, then stir in the onion mixture and simmer gently for 10 minutes. Ladle into warmed bowls and serve immediately, garnished with snipped chives.

Serves 6

1 tbsp sunflower oil

1 large onion, thinly sliced

2 garlic cloves, finely chopped

* 1.7 litres/3 pints basic vegetable stock

1½ tbsp red miso paste

1 tbsp tomato purée

1 tsp ground ginger

1 tsp ground coriander

2 carrots, thinly sliced

3 sheets yaki-nori seaweed (seasoned and toasted nori seaweed), torn into shreds

snipped fresh chives, to garnish

93

Crab Soup-Vietnam

1. Put the mushrooms into a bowl, pour in the water and leave to soak for 20 minutes. Meanwhile, chop the white parts of the spring onions and thinly slice the green parts diagonally. Slice the asparagus diagonally into 2-cm/¾-inch pieces. Pick over the crabmeat and remove any pieces of shell and cartilage.

2. Drain the mushrooms, reserving the soaking liquid, and squeeze gently to remove the excess liquid. Remove and discard the stalks and thinly slice the caps. Strain the soaking liquid through a muslin-lined strainer.

3. Heat the oil in a large saucepan. Add the chopped spring onions and garlic and stir-fry over a medium heat for 2 minutes. Pour in the stock and reserved soaking liquid, add the mushrooms and bring to the boil.

4. Stir in 1 tablespoon of the Thai fish sauce, add the sliced spring onions and asparagus pieces and bring back to the boil. Reduce the heat and simmer for 5 minutes, then gently stir in the crabmeat and coriander. Simmer for a further 3–4 minutes to heat through.

5. Remove the pan from the heat, taste and stir in more fish sauce, if necessary. Ladle into warmed bowls and serve immediately.

Serves 6

6 dried shiitake mushrooms

350 ml/12 fl oz hot water

5 spring onions

350 g/12 oz asparagus spears, trimmed

750 g/1 lb 10 oz white crabmeat, thawed if frozen

2 tbsp groundnut oil

3 garlic cloves, finely chopped

* 1.7 litres/3 pints basic vegetable stock

1–2 tbsp Thai fish sauce

3 tbsp chopped fresh coriander

Laksa–Malaysia

1 Peel the prawns, reserving the heads and shells. Devein the prawns by cutting a slit along their backs with a sharp knife and removing the black thread with the point of the knife. Rinse the heads and shells. Heat 1 tablespoon of the oil in a saucepan. Add the prawn heads and shells and stir-fry over a medium heat for 2–3 minutes, until lightly coloured, then pour in the stock and bring to the boil. Reduce the heat and simmer for 15 minutes. Strain the stock into a bowl and discard the prawn shells.

2 Mix together the curry paste and ground nuts in a bowl. Heat the remaining oil in a saucepan. Add the curry paste and cook over a low heat, stirring frequently, for 4–5 minutes, until the spices give off their aroma. Increase the heat to medium, pour in the stock and bring to the boil, then reduce the heat, cover and simmer for 20 minutes.

3 Meanwhile, put the noodles into a bowl, pour in boiling water to cover and leave to soak for 5 minutes, then drain. Blanch the beansprouts in boiling salted water for a few minutes, then drain. Whisk the coconut milk into the saucepan with the curry paste mixture and simmer for 2 minutes, then add the prawns, squid and sugar and season to taste with salt. Simmer for 5 minutes, until the prawns and squid are tender, then remove from the heat. Divide the noodles and beansprouts among warmed bowls and ladle the soup over them. Garnish with chopped coriander, cucumber strips and spring onions and serve immediately.

Serves 6

350 g/12 oz large raw prawns

6 tbsp groundnut oil

1.3 litres/2¼ pints basic vegetable stock

2 tbsp Panang curry paste (very hot) or red curry paste (hot)

25 g/1 oz candlenuts or cashews, ground

250 g/9 oz rice noodles

175 g/6 oz beansprouts

600 ml/1 pint canned coconut milk

175 g/6 oz prepared squid, scored and cut into small diamonds

1 tbsp soft brown sugar

salt

To garnish
chopped fresh coriander

cucumber, cut into julienne strips

chopped spring onions

Tom Yam Goong–Thailand

1. Peel the prawns, reserving the heads and shells. Devein the prawns by cutting a slit along their backs with a sharp knife and removing the black thread with the point of the knife. Rinse the heads and shells.

2. Pour the stock into a saucepan, add the prawn heads and tails, lemon grass, kaffir lime leaves and a pinch of salt and bring to the boil. Reduce the heat and simmer for 10 minutes. Strain the stock into a clean pan and discard the prawn shells.

3. Return the pan of stock to the heat, add the green chillies and bring back to the boil, then reduce the heat and simmer for a further 10 minutes. Stir in the Thai fish sauce and prawns and simmer for 5 minutes. Add the spring onions, lime juice and red chillies and heat through for 1–2 minutes.

4. Remove the pan from the heat and taste and adjust the seasoning with more lime juice or Thai fish sauce, if necessary. Ladle into warmed bowls, sprinkle with the coriander and serve immediately with the lime wedges.

Serves 6

500 g/1 lb 2 oz large raw prawns

* 1.5 litres/2¾ pints basic vegetable stock

3 lemon grass stalks bruised

6 kaffir lime leaves, torn

pinch of salt

3 green chillies, deseeded and thinly sliced

3 tbsp Thai fish sauce

3 spring onions, chopped

2 tbsp lime juice

2 red chillies, deseeded and thinly sliced

1 tbsp chopped fresh coriander, to garnish

lime wedges, to serve

96

Chicken Soup with Ginger & Coconut Milk—Thailand

1. Put the chicken, rice, lemon grass, garlic, chillies, lime leaves, ginger and coriander into a saucepan, pour in the stock and coconut milk and bring to the boil over a medium heat, stirring occasionally. Reduce the heat, cover and simmer for 1 hour.

2. Remove the pan from the heat and leave to cool slightly. Remove and discard the lemon grass and kaffir lime leaves. Ladle the soup into a food processor or blender, in batches if necessary, and process to a purée.

3. Return the soup to the rinsed-out pan, season to taste with salt and add the spring onions, corn cobs and mushrooms. Bring back to the boil, then reduce the heat and simmer for 5 minutes.

4. Remove the pan from the heat. Ladle the soup into warmed bowls, garnish with chopped coriander and chilli and serve immediately.

Serves 6

400 g/14 oz skinless, boneless chicken breasts, cut into strips

100 g/3½ oz Thai fragrant rice

1 lemon grass stalk, bruised

4 garlic cloves, roughly chopped

2 green chillies, deseeded and sliced

4 kaffir lime leaves, torn

2.5-cm/1-inch piece fresh ginger, chopped

4 tbsp chopped fresh coriander, plus extra to garnish

✳ 1.5 litres/2¾ pints basic vegetable stock

400 ml/14 fl oz canned coconut milk

4 spring onions, thinly sliced

115 g/4 oz baby corn cobs

115 g/4 oz button mushrooms, halved

salt

chopped red chilli, to garnish

Manhattan Clam Chowder—United States

1. Heat the oil in a saucepan. Add the salt pork and cook over a medium heat, stirring frequently, for 6–8 minutes, until golden brown. Remove with a slotted spoon.

2. Add the onion and celery to the pan, reduce the heat to low and cook, stirring occasionally, for 5 minutes, until softened. Increase the heat to medium, add the tomatoes, potatoes, thyme and parsley, return the pork to the pan, season with salt and pepper and pour in the tomato juice and stock. Bring to the boil, stirring constantly, then reduce the heat, cover and simmer for 15–20 minutes, until the potatoes are just tender.

3. Meanwhile, scrub the clams under cold running water. Discard any with broken shells or that do not shut when sharply tapped. Put them into a saucepan, pour in the wine, cover and cook over a high heat, shaking the pan occasionally, for 4–5 minutes, until the shells have opened.

4. Remove the clams with a slotted spoon and leave to cool slightly. Strain the cooking liquid through a muslin-lined strainer into the soup. Remove the clams from the shells.

5. Add the clams to the soup and heat through, stirring constantly, for 2–3 minutes. Remove from the heat and taste and adjust the seasoning, if necessary. Ladle into warmed bowls and serve immediately with crusty bread.

Serves 6

1 tsp sunflower oil

115 g/4 oz salt pork or unsmoked bacon, diced

1 onion, finely chopped

2 celery sticks, chopped

4 tomatoes, peeled, deseeded and chopped

3 potatoes, diced

pinch of dried thyme

3 tbsp chopped fresh parsley

150 ml/5 fl oz tomato juice

✳ 600 ml/1 pint basic vegetable stock

36 carpetshell or other small clams

150 ml/5 fl oz dry white wine

salt and pepper

crusty bread, to serve

Chicken & Corn Soup–United States

1. Remove the skin from the chicken, cut the meat off the bones and cut into small pieces. Put the saffron into a bowl, pour in hot water to cover and leave to soak.

2. Heat the oil in a saucepan. Add the onions and celery and cook over a low heat, stirring occasionally, for 5 minutes, until softened. Increase the heat to medium, pour in the stock, add the peppercorns and mace and bring to the boil. Reduce the heat and simmer for 25 minutes.

3. Increase the heat to medium, add the chicken, noodles, sweetcorn, sage, parsley and saffron with its soaking water, season to taste with salt and pepper and bring back to the boil. Reduce the heat and simmer for a further 20 minutes.

4. Remove the pan from the heat, taste and adjust the seasoning, if necessary, ladle into warmed bowls and serve immediately.

Serves 6

1 roasted chicken, about 1.3 kg/3 lb
½ tsp saffron threads
3 tbsp corn oil
2 onions, thinly sliced
3 celery sticks, sliced
1.7 litres/3 pints basic vegetable stock
8 black peppercorns
1 mace blade
115 g/4 oz egg noodles
400 g/14 oz frozen sweetcorn
pinch of dried sage
2 tbsp chopped fresh parsley
salt and pepper

99

Jamaican Pepper Pot–Caribbean

1. Put the steak, pork and callaloo into a large saucepan, pour in the stock and bring to the boil over a medium heat. Reduce the heat and simmer for 2–2¼ hours, until the meat is tender. Meanwhile, cut off the stems of fresh okra, if using, taking care not to pierce the pods. Dip the cut ends into salt and leave to drain in a colander for 30 minutes. Rinse well in water mixed with the lemon juice. If using frozen okra, rinse in water mixed with the lemon juice.

2. To make the plantain crisps, using a sharp knife, cut through the plantain skins along the ridges and peel off. Cut the flesh into wafer-thin slices with a mandoline or very sharp knife, put into a bowl of iced water and leave to soak for 30 minutes. Heat the oil in a deep-fryer to 180–190°C/ 350–375°F or until a cube of day-old bread browns in 30 seconds. Drain the plantain slices and pat dry with a tea towel. Dust with the cinnamon, add to the hot oil, in batches if necessary, and cook until golden brown. Remove with a slotted spoon and drain on kitchen paper.

3. Add the okra, sweet potato, christophine, chilli, coconut milk and spring onions to the pan, season with salt and pepper and bring back to the boil. Simmer for 35–40 minutes, until all the vegetables are tender and the soup has thickened. Remove the pan from the heat and taste and adjust the seasoning, if necessary. Ladle into warmed bowls and serve immediately, with the plantain crisps.

Serves 6

225 g/8 oz stewing steak, diced

225 g/8 oz salt pork, diced

225 g/8 oz callaloo or spinach, coarse stalks removed, finely chopped

2.8 litres/5 pints basic vegetable stock

225 g/8 oz fresh or frozen okra

1 tbsp lemon juice

225 g/8 oz sweet potato, sliced

225 g/8 oz christophine (chayote), peeled and thinly sliced

1 green chilli, deseeded and sliced

700 ml/1¼ pints canned coconut milk

2 spring onions, finely chopped

salt and pepper

Plantain crisps

2 plantains

iced water

vegetable oil, for deep-frying

ground cinnamon, for dusting

100

Black Bean Soup–Caribbean

1. Heat the oil in a large saucepan. Add the onion, celery and garlic and cook over a low heat, stirring occasionally, for 6–8 minutes, until softened.

2. Increase the heat to medium, add the beans, pour in the stock and bring to the boil. Reduce the heat, cover and simmer for 2–2½ hours, until the beans are tender.

3. Remove the pan from the heat and leave to cool slightly. Ladle all or half the soup, depending on the texture you require, into a food processor or blender, in batches if necessary, and process to a purée.

4. Return the soup to the pan and bring just to the boil. If it is very thick, add a little more stock or water. Stir in the cayenne pepper, lemon juice, vinegar, sherry and hard-boiled eggs and season to taste with salt and pepper. Reduce the heat and simmer, stirring constantly, for 10 minutes.

5. Remove the pan from the heat and ladle the soup into warmed bowls. Garnish with celery leaves and serve immediately, sprinkled with grated Cheddar cheese.

Serves 6

3 tbsp corn oil

1 large onion, chopped

2 celery sticks, chopped

2 garlic cloves, chopped

450 g/1 lb dried black beans or black-eyed beans, soaked overnight in cold water to cover, and drained

2.5 litres/4½ pints basic vegetable stock

¾ tsp cayenne pepper

5 tbsp lemon juice

2 tbsp red wine vinegar

2 tbsp dry sherry

4 hard-boiled eggs, roughly chopped

salt and pepper

chopped celery leaves, to garnish

grated Cheddar cheese, to serve